Tucker Lake
Chronicle

Tucker Lake Chronicle

Thirteen Months in the North Woods

Joan Crosby

NODIN PRESS

ISBN: 978-1-947237-17-9

Library of Congress control number: 2019900630

ACKNOWLEDGMENTS
A hearty thanks to the ghosts of Al, the Gunflint Lake guide, Will and Kermit of Loon Lake Lodge, and their father, Henning. My year in the woods was greatly enhanced by their hospitality, wilderness knowledge, and eccentricities.

A sincere thank you also goes out to my writing buddy of twenty years, Ann Mershon, who's been my cheerleader and sounding board and done a heck of a lot of editing.

A warm thank you to Faith Sullivan and her Mentorship in Fiction Writing class that inspirited me to do "one more rewrite." Faith's generous help to writers is unsurpassed.

I'm also grateful for the continued support and comaraderie from the other writers in the mentorship class: Judy Budreau, Soshanna Matney, Nina Simonowicz, Shelley Odendahl, and Sandy Bloom. I owe a special thanks to Nina and Soshanna for their help. Thank you to Norton Stillman of Nodin Press for having faith in me and to John Toren, whose editing skills continue to amaze me.

As always, I'm grateful to my husband, Dick, for his honesty and his steadfast support.

Nodin Press
5114 Cedar Lake Road
Minneapolis, MN 55416

www.nodinpress.com

Printed in USA

To my husband, Dick,
who started the whole thing!

Our chief mode of transport between the cabin and the road was an aluminum canoe powered by a four-horsepower outboard motor.

Contents

Tucker Lake

Chronicle

Dick and I at the cabin's front door.

PROLOGUE

I was a city girl. Not in my wildest dreams did I imagine I would give up my miniskirts and go-go boots to spend a year in a tiny one-room cabin in the northern Minnesota wilderness. By my early twenties, I had graduated from the University of Minnesota, landed a teaching job in the suburbs, and married my sweetheart. We were a typical middle-class couple on a path to fulfilling the American Dream—a four-bedroom colonial-style house in Edina complete with three children, two dogs, and a cat.

I enjoyed eating at good restaurants, followed the latest fashions, and felt proud at the sight of the Minneapolis skyline. But I also loved the outdoors. Until I turned fourteen, everyone called me a tomboy. I climbed trees, outraced boys, and never turned down a dare.

My outdoor self was placated by occasional outings to property Dick and I had purchased on Tucker Lake, in a remote area of northeastern Minnesota near the Gunflint Trail. Together we built a tiny cabin there, and we made the long drive north several times every year for weekend retreats. I enjoyed these outings but loudly declared I'd never live in a small town.

Then it happened. On a crazy impulse we decided to chuck our city life and spend not just a weekend, but a year in our tiny cabin on Tucker.

Family and friends didn't expect us to act on this wild plan, and when we did, they were confident we wouldn't stick it out for an entire year, but failure never occurred to us. If I did experience a twinge of apprehension, it quickly faded as our plans solidified. Dick and I were ready for an adventure. In September 1969 we packed up our lives and headed for Tucker Lake.

This is the story of our lives during that incredible year.

1

INSANITY

It was two o'clock in the afternoon. We had arrived at our wilderness cabin on Tucker Lake only a few hours earlier. I stood on the rocky shoreline of nearby Little Iron Lake, surrounded by spruce and birch, trying to suppress the nameless dread that filled the pit of my stomach. How had I gotten myself into this? Why had I ever agreed to such insanity? Trying to focus on the surrounding beauty, I concentrated on the occasional breeze ruffling the rust-colored water. It did no good. My heart still pounded. I took a deep breath, inhaling deeply of the pine-scented air. Nothing. Dark thoughts still filled my head. The wilderness seemed to close in, heavy and ominous.

Where was Dick? He'd been gone too long.

I peered down the lakeshore hoping to see his familiar form steering our boat around the rock-covered point. But there was nothing. I frowned. The sunny day had turned gray with a looming, lowering sky. Nooky, our Malamute puppy, restive and straining at her leash, seemed to sense my mood and growled low in her throat.

As I waited for Dick to appear, I thought back to the November day that brought me here. Dick and I had nursed our coffee that Sunday morning, looking across the breakfast table at each other. As a raw wind rattled dead leaves against our basement apartment windows, he had uttered the words that would change our lives.

"There has to be a better way to live."

His words electrified the air. "I couldn't agree more," I replied.

"Like spending a winter at the cabin," Dick continued. "Wouldn't that be fun?"

"Whoa. That might be a little much." I answered. "Suburban life might be dull, but do we really want to spend a winter roughing it under arctic conditions?"

Now this conversation came back to me, and I knelt and gave Nooky a hug. As I continued to search the lakeshore for Dick, I remembered I'd told him that I wasn't sure I could handle a year without running water or electricity, but was willing to explore the idea.

"Let's go up to the Gunflint Trail in January, see what it's like," Dick said, "and then make our decision."

We spent a weekend at Loon Lake Lodge, snowmobiling, snowshoeing, enjoying the sparkling white snow-covered lakes. Temperatures were moderate and the snow was clean and glistening, unlike the often dirty slush in Minneapolis.

We returned to our little apartment in Plymouth filled with enthusiasm. I told Dick, "I'm willing to have an adventure, live in our cabin for a winter. The snow was so clean up there…the temperatures weren't that bad…"

Happy and excited, we began making plans, and I told anyone who'd listen about Joan and Dick's Great Adventure.

Now, here I was. Alone in the woods, forty miles from town with dark thoughts circling in my head. Dick should have been back long before now. What had we done?

2

The Adventure Begins

We had left Minneapolis at a chilly two o'clock A.M. looking like ragtag gypsies. Our blue and white Bronco was loaded with so much gear it was a wonder the taillights weren't dragging. Jeans, jackets, sweatshirts and underwear, a two-month food supply—all the paraphernalia of our new life was either inside or on top of the car. We'd even remembered to bring Nooky's favorite toy, a pink rubber ladybug.

In 1969 there was no freeway between the Twin Cities and Duluth, and the journey between Minneapolis and the Gunflint Trail was a long, dull, eight-hour drive. I was excited when we finally reached Little Iron Lake, the point of access to our cabin's more remote location on Tucker Lake. We unloaded an astounding amount of "stuff" into the canoe that we kept at the landing. We were now only one portage away from our new life.

The next step was for Dick to motor the overladen canoe down the shore of Little Iron while I drove the same distance and parked the Bronco near a second landing where he would pick me up. Easy-peasy. I'd hop in the boat already loaded to the gunnels, and we'd cross the lake to the portage leading to Tucker Lake and our cabin.

I'd parked the car, and now Nooky and I waited at our meeting place. But Dick was nowhere in sight. This was scary. He should have been here. I thought of those gunnels riding very close to the waterline.

Several cold drops of rain spattered my face as I listened in vain for the sound of a boat motor. I glanced at the darkening sky, and the enormity of the wilderness suddenly struck. I was alone. No telephone. The nearest hospital or doctor was forty miles away, and we still had the rest of Little Iron, a muddy 300-foot portage, and three miles of Tucker Lake to cross before reaching our cabin.

A shiver crept down my spine. Where was Dick?

Again, I thought back to the past few months.

During the summer of 1969, while the Apollo astronauts landed on the moon and Woodstock was a "happening," Dick and I quit our jobs, bought a Malamute puppy with mischievous brown eyes, and, because our apartment lease was up, moved into my parents' upstairs bedroom for the summer. We counted our pennies. I even taught summer school to pad our account.

Finally, with only $1,100 in savings (far short of our goal), we lost patience. "The heck with it—we'll work it out," we said, and headed north.

Now here I was, worried, tired, and hungry. Nooky sensed my nervousness and squirmed on her leash, ears pricked, alert.

I had almost lost my battle to stay calm when a faint noise reverberated somewhere to the east.

Over my fears, I stopped panicking and listened, cocking an ear. Was it Dick? Straining to hear, I didn't move a muscle. It might be. I crossed my fingers and held my breath, hoping the distant sound would get louder. It could be. Was it?

Yes. It was. The heartwarming, reassuring sound of a boat motor filled the air, and I gave a huge sigh of relief as our small vessel, loaded with gear and Dick, duck hat and all, putt-putted

We built the original one-room cabin in 1966 as a vacation spot. Dick and a friend brought in the materials via snowmobile during the winter.

around the point. It was the most welcome sight I'd seen in a long time.

"Sorry I took so long," he told me as he pulled the boat to shore, "but the canoe is so overloaded, I had to go slow."

"I was worried about you," I said as I climbed into the vessel. "But all that matters now is that we're together and our adventure has truly begun!"

The job that still lay ahead of us that afternoon was gargantuan. Once we'd crossed the lake, we'd have to unload everything from the canoe, lug it across the portage, reload it into the canoe, and unload it all once again when we reached the cabin. It would surely be dusk when we finally arrived.

꙳

Two hours later, as I opened the door to our little lakeside cabin, tired but also giddy with excitement, I was greeted by a musty smell, and as my eyes adjusted to the dark I was shocked to see that the plywood floor was covered with splintered glass.

"Oh no," I groaned.

Behind me, Dick's voice was edgy with exhaustion. "What?"

"The floor!" My own voice quavered. I slowly inched my way farther inside the small building. "The floor!" My eyes moved across the floor and up to the wall behind the Coleman cooking stove where window glass should have been. But wasn't. "The window behind the stove is broken!" I yelled. "Get in here!"

Carrying a huge Duluth pack filled with foodstuffs, Dick pulled himself swiftly up the steps and rushed into the cabin.

"What the —!" Baffled, he stepped around the broken glass to stand beside me. We surveyed the tiny room: the bunk beds were intact, the plywood shelf under the east window was in place, but the window itself was shattered. No barrier protected us from the dark shadows of the fathomless woods beyond the window and all that they hid.

"Let's take a look outside," Dick said. I followed, shivering with cold, fear, and weariness. It was seven o'clock, and the sunlight was nearly gone. We'd been up for a long time. My stomach growled, my bones ached. All I wanted was a meal and a soft pillow.

Dick rounded the cabin corner and disappeared. I hesitated. Suddenly his voice pierced the air. "Come here!" His tone sent chills down my spine.

Dick's flashlight flooded the cabin's back wall, illuminating several long deep gouges in the plywood. I gasped. Dick moved the beam higher, exposing one very large paw print. Moving the beam farther still revealed more paw marks, all imprinted in blood. Bear paws. And, judging from the size of the paws, the intruder was big—very big.

"But what the heck attracted a bear?" I said. We never left anything in the cabin that might pique a bear's interest. Not crumb of food. And we always scoured every kitchen utensil spotlessly clean before leaving.

Jumpy with exhaustion, we trudged back inside and conducted a thorough investigation, inspecting every inch of the little cabin. We found nothing. Not a forgotten Ritz cracker, not a packet of dried Lipton's Noodle Soup. Nada.

A spooky silence filled the small room. Was the bear somewhere nearby? Then Dick said, "Here's the problem." He held up a yellow plastic scouring pad. "Has to be. See! It's got hidden grease."

Dumbfounded, I stared at a few teensy remnants hiding deep in the interior of the plastic strands. "*That* tiny amount attracted a bear?" I gulped, overwhelmed, suddenly realizing how little I really knew about the wilderness.

Now that the mystery was solved, I felt a surge of energy and helped Dick unload and carry gear to the cabin in the waning light with enthusiasm. Then I swept up the broken glass and heated a packet of soup while Dick covered the open window with clear plastic.

Sitting on duffel bags and Duluth packs, we spooned down cups of split pea soup. Within minutes, we were nourished and relaxed, and exhaustion set in again. We unrolled our sleeping bags without a word and spread toothpaste on toothbrushes, making ready for bed. We were too beat to talk.

I slipped into cotton pajamas and followed Dick outside to brush my teeth and spit into the underbrush. I was gargling, making a racket, when Dick raised a finger to his lips.

"Shhh..."He hissed

I froze. An eerie wailing sing-song noise, punctuated by huffing, sounded from the east.

"Bear?" I whispered.

Dick nodded. "I think so."

The hair on the back of my neck stood up. I was in the wilderness with a wild animal approaching, one possibly familiar with our cabin. If a bear had been interested in a tiny amount of grease in a scouring pad, how attractive would our cabin be now with its large cache of food?

Trying to squelch rampaging fear, I thought, *This is part of*

Dick and Joan's Great Adventure. Why am I panicking? Take a deep breath and quit being silly. Dick had a shotgun. We weren't in any real danger.

With a jolt, I experienced an insight: I like this excitement. The bear's presence, the dark night, the deep forest were all scary but exhilarating. This was better than lolling in front of the TV in our drab city apartment. This was adventure. Holding my breath, I listened to the night, and my fear melted away.

And now it seemed that rather than wailing, the bear was singing. Funny I hadn't realized before. It was a peculiar but enthralling sound. The creature didn't know we had moved into his territory—not yet. The strange chanting moved close. And closer.

"I'll fire the shotgun in the air if he gets too close," Dick whispered. I nodded but didn't really want the bear song to end. I imagined a large furry creature lumbering carelessly along the lake shore, unaware that humans were listening.

Then the noise stopped. We froze. Had the bear caught our scent? We strained our ears. A small animal rustled in the underbrush. Something jumped into the lake, making a splash, but nothing wailed and nothing huffed. No bear noises. We listened one, two, five minutes. No chuffing or grunting.

The bear was gone.

We slept soundly that night thanks to excitement, exhaustion, and heavy doses of fresh air. My last thought before falling asleep was, *This is going to be an exciting year.*

3

New Routines

Remember that wonderful feeling of freedom you experienced as a kid on the first day of summer vacation? That's how I felt the next morning as the pure blue sky, the sweet scent of pine, and the soft lapping waves of Tucker Lake greeted me through the tiny window next to my bunk. I got up, shimmied into my jeans and pulled a sweatshirt over my head, then walked over to take a look out the front window at Tucker Lake.

Our cabin sat atop a small knoll with a towering white pine behind its northeast corner and the long narrow waters of Tucker Lake only a few feet beyond the front door. Tucker is three miles long and a quarter mile wide at its widest—more like a river than a lake. Our cabin was situated at the widest point in the westerly half, directly across from a peninsula and two small islands. The main segment of the lake lay to our east.

Tucker was a great walleye fishing lake in those days, and both locals and guests from nearby lodges often spent weekend days fishing there. During our year-long adventure, we were the lake's only permanent inhabitants, although Dick's high school friend and his wife owned a cabin toward the end of the lake, about half a mile west of ours.

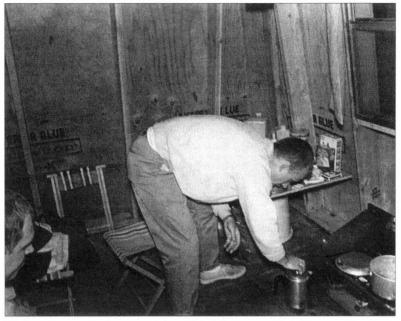

Dick makes coffee in our original "kitchen," a small shelf extending from the wall and a Coleman camping stove. The window above Dick's head is the one we found smashed in by a bear upon our arrival.

On that first morning, with thoughts of bears and broken glass behind me, I trotted cheerily out to the "bathroom"—a platform covering a hole in the ground—then joined Dick as we washed our faces in the cold, clear waters of the lake. I fixed a hearty breakfast, and we sat on the bottom bunk, holding camping plates on our laps, as we gobbled crisp bacon and eggs fried over-easy.

I'd like to report that we meditated on the beauty of the day, exchanging lofty words and thoughts, but the truth was, we were eager to get moving, so our chatter was practical. There was a lot to do before our little cabin would be fit for winter. This was Dick's overriding concern, but I also wanted to "cute" up our tiny cubicle and make it a cozy little place in the woods.

At the time, our new home resembled a storage dump, with little free space to move or put things amid piles of tools, yards of rolled fiberglass insulation, books, duffel bags crammed with clothes, cleaning products, and even a kitchen sink we hoped to install. Measuring twelve feet square, the cabin wasn't much bigger than a tree house. Dick had built a set of bunk beds on the west wall; under a small window on the north wall sat a large brown plastic garbage can alongside two smaller green ones filled with winter clothes, bedding, and food. In the northeast corner a piece of plywood fastened to the wall served as a cooking area. A Coleman cook stove sat on a built-in shelf below the broken window on the east wall, and a small, cast-iron, wood-burning sweetheart stove filled the southeast corner. Only the window overlooking the lake on the south wall saved us from utter claustrophobia, though a muddle of tools, boxes, rope coils, and paint cans was spread out under it.

We needed to create order out of this chaos, and our morning conversation dwelt on chores. It was exciting to make plans, dream of the future. Over a cup of throat-searing coffee, Dick decided that his top priority would be to insulate the southeast corner of the cabin so we could replace our old stove with a more attractive and efficient Franklin fireplace. I took on the task of digging a garbage pit.

My hopes were high when I started. Planting the spade tip as far in the ground as possible, I pushed down with my foot, throwing my whole weight behind it. The result? Nothing but beads of sweat on my brow and an ominous metallic chink as the shovel hit rock. *Keep going*, I told myself. *You can do it*. Readjusting the spade under the rock, I gave another hard downward thrust, then wriggled and rocked the spade. Nothing. *Don't give up*, I chided myself. On the point of despair, I gave the spade a third thrust and pried loose a single medium-size rock.

Leaning on the handle of the spade, I thought wistfully of the black loam in my mother's Minneapolis garden. Under a thin layer of humus, this northern Minnesota stuff was rocks,

rocks, and more rocks—a vast underworld of pebbles, stones, and mini-boulders.

Although the September day was pleasant, with moose maple glowing red and birch trees flashing yellow, I soon became glum. And after an hour of digging, I'd succeeded in making only a shallow depression in the forest floor—not much to show for all that effort.

At one point Nooky stopped chasing red squirrels long enough to investigate my progress. Her plumed tail wagging, she sniffed at the small pile of rocks I'd built up, then vigorously pawed it, sending a barrage of loose humus and pebbles flying at me.

"Could you cooperate, just a bit?" I scolded as the rocks and vines landed at my feet. But at that moment she spotted another squirrel and scampered away in hot pursuit. When she returned a few minutes later a glob of squirrel poop rested on her black-masked forehead.

"Dick!" I called. "Get outside and take a look at Nooky. She's been chasing squirrels. You won't believe it!"

He stepped out the door. "This had better be good..." His voice trailed off and ended in a loud peal of laughter as he looked at our naïve puppy. Nooky, oblivious to the humiliation we were heaping on her, pranced proudly, believing she had bested the squirrels. She leaped off into the brush at the sound of squirrel chattering, happy as could be, and we returned to our tasks.

I twisted the shovel under a root and scrabbled out a few more rocks. The job wasn't easy, but we needed this garbage pit. Dick was working hard inside the cabin on the winterizing, and I had to hold up my end of our partnership. Besides, this was only the beginning. When the garbage pit was finished, my next project would be to dig a cistern.

The sound of a stapler pinged through the crisp autumn air again and again as Dick fastened fiberglass insulation to the cabin's southeast corner. I was eager for him to finish so we could install a cement hearth for the Franklin fireplace. It would make our little home much cozier.

The thought that the two of us were alone in the woods, at the mercy of the elements and entirely dependent on each other, crossed my mind more than once, but it didn't unsettle me. The sound of the stapler, the thunk of my shovel, and the crash of branches as Nooky pursued squirrels became a forest ensemble that gave me a strange feeling of serenity as we worked at our appointed tasks.

4

KEEPING BUSY

When we mentioned our plan to spend a year in the remote reaches of the North Woods to friends, the question they asked most often was: "How will you take a shower?" Number two on the list was: "What will you do with all that spare time?"

Spare time wasn't a problem. After five days in the wilderness, Dick and I were hopping up and down like drops of water on a hot griddle, busy settling in, busy making future plans. *I never thought I'd have so much to do*, I reflected as I dipped a large plastic bucket into the rust-colored water of Tucker Lake. Iron ore caused the pale brownish color, but did not taint the water. We drank it straight from the lake without filtering or boiling and never suffered any consequences.

When the first pail was full, I plunged a second container under the surface and watched the bubbles rise as it filled. Then, picking up both vessels, I carefully lugged them the short distance to the cabin. The overcast gray sky lent a somber feel to the day, but the temperature was still warm, and my jeans and soft cotton sweatshirt felt just right as I placed the water containers on the small shelf Dick had built in the northeast cabin corner.

The original wood-burning stove. Note the lovely plywood décor.

Standing by the south window and looking out at the gray rock peninsula across the narrow stretch of lake fronting our cabin, I hoped to see a lumbering moose or wolf scrambling across the low cliffs that rose from the water on the opposite shore.

Spotting nothing, I pondered my next move, chuckling at the question many friends had asked me: Too much time on our hands? Ha!

One reason for our busyness was the lack of plumbing or electricity, without which the simple act of going to the bathroom, for example, becomes a chore. It begins with grabbing a roll of toilet paper and walking to the "outside" bathroom. Ours was neither an outhouse nor a privy, but merely a latrine—a platform over a hole in the ground. Washing hands after finishing the "job" wasn't a simple matter, either. Rather than simply turning a faucet for hot water, it involved going back to the cabin, pouring warm water from a stove-top container into a plastic tub, washing, then walking back outside to toss the dirty water into the underbrush.

As a result of activities like these, our pace of life slowed down. The day might be filled with chores, but we did them at our own pace, and I found it relaxing, while the physical activity gave me a sense of accomplishment and well-being.

The chores were numerous. No doubt about that. With no electricity, fueling the Coleman stove and kerosene lamps was a seemingly endless task. Lacking a furnace, we were required a maintain an ample supply of wood and keep the fire burning to maintain the cabin at a comfortable temperature. Also gone were the days of turning on the burner of an electric stove to cook meals. Now I had to make certain the Coleman stove was fueled, then pump up its pressure and light the burners. These tasks filled a good part of the day.

Some jobs that we thought would be difficult proved easy, while other seemingly simple chores developed into complicated undertakings.

We figured moving the heavy cast-iron Franklin fireplace would take all day, and I dreaded the very thought, but the opposite happened. Moving it inch by inch, we were able to transport the monster stove smoothly, setting it on the hearth in a short time. It looked so fine, shiny, and black with a cozy fire crackling in its fireplace, we poured glasses of Chianti and toasted our success.

∾

After five days setting up and getting used to our routines, I paused to contemplate the lifestyle changes we'd made. I stood at the window, mesmerized by the soft gray of lake and sky and the dark green of spruce trees, and considered my next chore. I knew what needed to be done, and I dreaded the thought—digging a cistern. I'd finished the garbage pit and a new outhouse hole, gritting my teeth, scooping up rock after rock, and finally completing the jobs. Digging a third hole in the ground shouldn't be that big of a deal. Yet I dreaded it.

We yearned for enough water for washing dishes, cleaning the cabin, even bathing, but that was proving difficult. Two separate digging efforts had had mixed results. One hole had yielded inadequate amounts of ground water. The other showed some promise; it was the only remaining hope.

Today I would dig at that hole. Dick would continue to spend his time as he had for the better part of the last few days, cutting firewood.

I turned from the window and braced myself for the chore I'd avoided all morning. After pulling on rubber boots and work gloves, I trudged outside, picked up the shovel, and went to the finish work on our last hope for a cistern.

The hole I'd dug was a scant ten feet from the cabin in the same clearing. It was a crumbling two feet in diameter and hardly four feet deep. I felt my stomach churn as I dropped into the narrow, muddy declivity. I dreaded this chore.

Stay positive, Joan! Trying to think of something optimistic, I honed in on the rrrring whine of Dick's chainsaw as he cut firewood on the far side of the cabin. The noise was comforting. It meant he was within shouting distance in case I got stuck in this infernal hole with my feet entombed by mud.

C'mon. Don't think that way. What could really go wrong? I stared at my feet, encased in olive green rubber boots and planted squarely in the hole's muddy bottom, which oozed with a sucking sound at the slightest movement. Was there such a thing as quicksand in the Superior National Forest? I didn't think so but couldn't stop from shifting my feet like a nervous pony.

The hole's narrow dimensions didn't leave much room for maneuvering or digging. Although I was only chest-deep and could scramble out, I felt trapped. With a heavy sigh, I began grubbing in the wet, clayey soil. It was impossible to fill more than a fourth of the shovel before standing up to empty it.

Otherwise it all fell back into the hole. How frustrating. There wasn't enough room to push the shovel deeper. I decided to scrape at the sides to make more elbow room, but the rock-and-vine-filled clay soil was too wet to hold its shape, and as I carved, small batches fell, covering my feet with more mud, sand, and gravel. With another deep sigh, I returned to my original task of digging. Deeper, not wider, was the only way.

The wet earth made each shovel feel like it weighed twenty-five pounds. Why, I wondered, did so much seepage exist, yet not enough to fill a well? To add to the dreary situation, the soft gray skies of an hour ago had turned dark, and raindrops were pattering down.

"Just what I need," I grumbled, wiping my face with a muck-covered glove.

Grimly, I stuck to my chore. Mud streaked my green rain pants and jacket. The rain fell in a light but chilling mist. I dug. My work gloves took on more and more water, until a clammy dampness encased my hands. Both my wide-brimmed rain hat and the red bandana I'd tied around my ears for warmth were soaked.

I dug, pushed, and shoveled with all my might, but only occasionally loosened a rock or muscled a tiny bit of soil onto the shovel. Up and down, scooping and lifting. Trying to keep the shovel contents from spilling back into the hole. Moving feet in the squishy mud. Throwing out one tiny shovel full, then another. Up and down. Pushing and lifting on and on and on.

Two hours had gone by in this way when suddenly, without warning, the entire rear wall of the hole crumbled, cascading to the bottom and completely decimating the day's work. I was heartsick. I had gotten nowhere. Tears filled my eyes.

I kept digging as mutinous thoughts grew. *What am I doing? Why didn't I quit an hour ago? This is a fool's task. Nothing will ever come of this.* With each shovel thrust, my anger and self-reproach grew.

Still trying to remain stoic, I controlled my seething emotions until the next shovelful exposed a massive area of wobbling pie plate–shaped rocks. My body went rigid. There was no question; they would cave in, bringing down a large area of soil. It was the final straw. I saw red.

"I'm done!" I screamed. "I don't care if this damn hole never gets dug. It's a waste of time, a dumb, stupid, useless thing to do!"

Crawling from the hole, mud-covered and tear-streaked, I threw the shovel as far as I could, hitting a small spruce tree with a clang, and ran into the cabin.

"And don't ask me to come back!" I yelled at the suddenly silent woods as the aggressive whine of Dick's chainsaw stopped.

Within minutes he returned to the cabin. "Are you all right?" His forehead wrinkled.

"I'm fine," I snapped, "but the cistern isn't, and I'm not discussing it either."

Dick said nothing, but went outside. He must have retrieved the thrown shovel since I heard it scrape as he pushed it into the ground. Was he trying to see if he could conquer that wet clay crappy soil? Probably. Well, good luck.

How would he fare? Feeling calmer, I sat on the bottom bunk and listened as he dug. Great. If he could dig out that damn hole, more power to him. I kept my ears tuned, but the sound of the digging soon stopped, to be replaced a few minutes later by the familiar buzz of the chainsaw. He, too, had given up.

We never talked about the cistern again.

5

THE RIDGE

We'd been in the woods for a mere week, but I felt I'd lived there much longer. Every day was chock full of chores and new experience. I loved my new life. Between chores, I often stared dreamily from the cabin window at the ridge across the lake, admiring the rich gold birch and dark green pines sprinkled along the rim. Now on the Sunday of our first week, we were off to explore it.

Dick pulled the canoe to shore, and we jumped onto the mossy ground. Nooky jumped from the canoe, too, and started running in circles, her plumed tail wagging. Dick had explored this area several years ago and discovered not just an overgrown old trail, but a well-used logging road. I could hardly believe it. Weren't we right next door to the BWCA*?

Dick led the way uphill, pointing out the three-foot-wide boundary line we were following as we trudged. There was no arguing the point—this was truly a survey line—but I was disappointed. I had enjoyed thinking of Tucker Lake as our private wilderness.

---

*Before the BWCA added a terminal W and became the BWCAW wilderness area in 1978, some sections of its periphery could be logged.

As I climbed the hill, my breathing was even and I felt strong. I was already in much better shape than a week ago when we first arrived. Stepping through the low swampy area near the lake was a bit tricky, but my newly strengthened legs climbed the ridge with surprising ease. The ground grew more firm and the trees larger, and we moved at a faster pace with no trouble.

Halfway up the hill, Dick pointed up and to the left where a large bird nest of sticks and branches filled the crook of a tree. Several years earlier, on one of our summer visits to Tucker, we had watched in amazement as a huge osprey swooped from sky to lake and scooped up a fish. "Could that be its nest?"

"We should get a bird book and look it up," Dick said.

We climbed for half a mile until, with a jolt, Dick stopped at the top of a small hill. I almost bumped into him. He pointed down the hill in front of us. Ten feet below was a well-kept gravel road with culverts. Judging from the recent imprint of tire tracks, this road was still in use and fairly well traveled.

I was speechless. What a disillusionment. While we were living the "wilderness life" a mere half a mile across the lake, people were driving vehicles back and forth through the woods. It's a wonder we never heard them.

I was twenty-six at the time, idealistic and naïve. "I thought the BWCA was protected from mechanical stuff," I said.

Dick explained. "It is, for the most part. But right here on the fringe, a few logging roads are allowed so loggers can harvest private tracts farther inland. These roads aren't open to the public, but nobody says we can't walk on them. Come on!"

We explored for the next hour, stopping to examine the huge hoof prints of a moose, the scat piles left by bear, and an occasional wolf track, the size of a large dog's, which Nooky cautiously sniffed.

"Wild animals seem to like walking on manmade roads," I commented.

We ambled west on this pleasant sunny day, thinking we might see a critter, or that the end of the road might be in sight, or that something exciting would happen. Nothing changed. The road stretched on and on to the west. Finally, we turned around.

Wagging her tail as we circled, Nooky eagerly bounded towards home. I assumed she was feeling the same hunger pangs I was. I'd forgotten to bring lunch, and it was now midafternoon. We started walking faster and had just reached the small hill where the surveyor line met the logging road when I felt a chill in the air.

I looked up. "Uh-oh!" A bank of black clouds was rolling in from the north. Nooky gave a low growl as thunder boomed.

"Can we make it to the cabin before the storm?" I shouted.

"Don't know, but let's get out of here!" Dick yelled. "Go! Run!" Scrambling down the path, tripping and stumbling on roots and rocks, we finally reached the canoe. We leaped in, pushed off, and Dick got our little four-horsepower motor going. Would we make it across the lake before the storm broke? A crack of lightning on the opposite shore told us we wouldn't. And crossing even a narrow body of water in a storm is never a good idea.

As lightning flashed furiously and thunder pealed in loud booms, we clung to some overhanging branches to hold the canoe close to shore. Soon the rain was falling in sheets. We were safe but getting wetter by the moment. Nooky's thick fluffy Malamute fur became plastered to her body, shrinking her size. She looked miserable and disgusted.

Our clothes turned sodden. My pigtails dripped and raindrops fell from Dick's duck hat. We soon reached the point where we couldn't have gotten any wetter, and I was wondering how long we were going to be trapped here, when the sky began to brighten. As quickly as it had arrived, the storm dissipated. The sheet of dark clouds continued south and east, to be followed by a more benign cloud cover. Within minutes the crashing thunder became a distant rumble, and lightning flickered at a safe distance. The storm had moved on.

But it left a cold rain in its place. And who could say what the next half hour might bring? We weren't taking any chances. Dick started the motor, and we sped across the lake.

With chattering teeth and soaking wet clothes, we tied the canoe to our little log dock and ran for the cabin's warmth. Once inside, Dick revived the coals in the fireplace with a few pieces of kindling, then threw several logs on the fire. We changed into dry clothes, and I brewed a pot of strong coffee. Nooky preferred to stay outside, crawling under the cabin to snuggle in her cozy burrow where she kept her favorite toy, the pink ladybug.

Soon we were drinking steaming hot coffee in front of a crackling fire. As my numb fingers warmed and the heat of the fire dried my soaked hair, I realized I'd learned a lot. Things weren't always as you imagined, like a logging road in a wilderness, and all the wealth in the world couldn't purchase anything more wonderful than a warm, safe shelter.

I also learned never again to forget rain gear. Anywhere. Anytime.

6

BAKING, BUILDING, AND BATHING

After ten days in the wilderness, I was beginning to feel as if I'd always lived here. Today promised to be busy. Noting that the fireplace embers glowed deep red, a perfect bread-baking temperature, I moved to the kitchen table and lifted the lid of the Dutch oven, revealing two shiny balls of sourdough. Were they ready to bake? I pinched a tiny portion, and my imprint remained. They were.

The two loaves had risen beautifully, so, setting aside the lid—bread bakes better in direct heat—I opened the fireplace doors, pulled out an iron grate, and gently positioned the Dutch oven on top of it. My last step was to carefully swing the grate directly over the embers where the raw dough would be transformed into golden brown loaves permeated by a delicious wood fire flavor.

When we started the Tucker Lake adventure, my plan was to do lots of home baking to save money, but I never considered sourdough bread, figuring I'd buy yeast packets at the grocery store. Then I read an article in *Mother Earth News* that gave specific directions for making and keeping sourdough starter. It didn't sound hard. I was suddenly filled with enthusiasm. Why not make my own starter? After all, the nearest store was forty miles away.

Following the instructions, I stirred a tablespoon of store-bought yeast, a cup of flour, a teaspoon of sugar, and some Tucker Lake water in an empty jam jar and set it in a warm spot. I didn't truly expect this experiment to work but was delighted to be wrong. Within a few days the small batch of sourdough was bubbling with fermentation, and I baked my first batch of true sourdough bread. As long as I kept adding flour and water, this homemade yeast supply would be available indefinitely. As an added bonus, I found that the flavor grew better every time I used my own starter.

As the bread baked that day, it filled the cabin with a rich, nutty aroma. Satisfied with having gotten that chore underway, I stepped over to the new kitchen table that Dick had built under the east window, where two unbaked apple pies rested on a red-checked tablecloth. I planned to bake the pies on the grate when the bread was done, protected from ashes by a covering of aluminum foil. The result, I hoped, would be two pies with flaky golden crusts, oozing with juicy filling. It worked! A surge of pride flushed my face as I thought about my baking successes. But I was eager to move on to the rest of my chores.

Today's bustling had a purpose. Company would be visiting for the next two weekends. Dick's parents were arriving tomorrow, and my sister and her husband the following week. I was in a tizzy, wanting the cabin to be presentable. Our little home was cramped, but I figured at the very least it should be cozy, and the food good.

While I baked, Dick upgraded our tiny abode. He tore down the old bunks and replaced them with a fancy new double bunk bed against the north wall. The top bunk was hinged, so we could lift it up and latch it against the wall. The lower bunk then served as a sitting place during the day and our bed at night.

He also built a four-shelf storage closet in the northeast corner where my small work table once stood, and I'd covered it with a hand-stitched curtain made from sale fabric purchased at Joynes department store in Grand Marais.

With blankets, clothing, and even canned foods stored neatly in my new pantry, our little home was a darn sight more welcoming than it had been the day of our arrival. I felt a flash of pride every time I stepped through the door. Everything in it had been produced by our efforts and ours alone.

One major task remained before company arrived: we needed to bathe. In the short time we'd lived here, we'd gotten in the habit of sponge bathing every morning. However, we soon learned that that method had its limits, and we'd designated Saturday nights as "bath night," but with company arriving we were forced to break the routine.

Once we'd finished our evening meal of homemade bread, thick vegetable soup, and apple pie, we began the whole bath process. First we toted a thirty-gallon green plastic garbage can down to the lake and filled it with as much water as we could carry. Bringing it inside the cabin, we scooped water from it into our two cooking pots and heated it on the wood stove. Once the water was heated, we emptied it into a second garbage can and slapped on a lid to keep it warm. It took more than an hour to fill it with an adequate amount for a bath.

The next step was the fun part.

Everything went smooth as silk as I stepped into our makeshift tub. The cabin was toasty warm, and although I couldn't sit the way you do in a real tub, if I hunkered down, twisted and turned, I could splash enough water on myself to get squeaky clean.

Finally, I stepped out onto some soft rugs I'd placed on the floor and dried off with a towel while Dick took his turn. We had extra water heating on the stove, which I poured over his back.

The whole procedure took almost two hours, and water got splashed on the floor, the bottom bunk, and even the kitchen table, but the result was well worth it. The cabin was warm, my skin glowed, and I swear I'd never felt cleaner in my entire life.

7

COMPANY OF ALL KINDS

Tears pricked my eyelids as our small aluminum boat sped across the rust-colored water of Little Iron Lake. Fiercely, I rubbed them. What was the matter with me? Ten minutes earlier, we had said good-bye to my sister and her husband after a weekend visit. As I watched their car disappear down the Gunflint Trail, I had been hit with a sudden surge of loneliness.

For several weeks we'd been bustling and busy. Dick's parents had visited the previous weekend, and despite the extra cooking and water-hauling, camaraderie and laughter had filled our small cabin.

A day or two later, after we made a hurried trip to Grand Marais to wash sleeping bags and sheets at the laundromat, my sister and her husband arrived. The men fished. My sister and I caught up on gossip. I loved showing off my new life, and everyone was a good sport about our cramped quarters.

Suddenly this visit, too, was over, and now, as we motored back to the cabin, I was overwhelmed by a fierce longing for Minneapolis. The image of our small, bare-walled cabin filled my mind. *It'll be so lonely there.* I missed Mom and Dad, and shopping at Byerlys. I missed my sister. Heck, I missed everything I'd left behind. What I wouldn't give for a shiny tiled bathroom and nice hot shower.

Tears ran down my cheeks, and I turned my face to hide them. Then I heard Dick suck in his breath. "Look!" he whispered, pointing. We had almost reached the small opening in the trees and underbrush that was our portage path. I gasped.

Directly ahead of us, in the spot where we always landed the boat, loomed the bulky brown body of a huge bull moose. His enormous rack rose majestically from his massive head. His giant hooves were sunk into the mud of the path where, not an hour ago, we had stood with my sister and her husband as we brought them to their car on the Gunflint Trail. The enormous creature was blocking our path.

Contemplating us, he held his huge head and massive snout steady, the pendant below his throat quivering slightly. My breath caught as Dick cut the motor and grabbed an oar, which he quietly used to bring the boat to a stop and keep it from floating too close to shore.

Moose sometimes make snorting sounds, but this one stood still and silent, watching us. He was magnificent—long-legged and with a deep chest, much bigger than the draft horses I'd seen in parades. His large nostrils moved as he took in our scent.⁻

One minute stretched into two, then three, as the moose watched us and we stared back in utter silence. Then, as if tiring of us, he turned his massive head and moved ponderously away, his huge haunches rippling with muscles as he slowly crashed into the forest.

We had no choice but to land at the very spot on which he'd stood and cross the narrow neck of land to the canoe stashed at the other end of the portage. It was our only route home. But it didn't feel safe. "I'm not thrilled at the idea of walking on our path," I said. "Do you think he's really gone?"

Dick shrugged. "What else can we do? He seems to be."

"I suppose we'd hear him if he came near?" I was doubtful.

"We can't sit here forever."

"I know."

"Remember always to keep a tree between you and a moose," Dick said with a chuckle.

I stared at him, flabbergasted.

"That's what everyone says," he added nonchalantly.

We approached shore slowly, Dick steering with an oar. We weren't in a hurry. When the boat's hull finally touched land with a gentle bump, we continued to sit silently, straining to hear snapping twigs, cawing crows, and more "moose sounds." The portage was quiet. Was the moose nearby? Probably not, but we couldn't be certain. I eyeballed Dick anxiously.

Bull moose can weigh as much as 1,200 pounds and are unusually aggressive during rutting season. It was rutting season.

"Nothing we can do but get out and walk across the portage," Dick said finally. "We get to the other side, hop in our canoe, and we're home free."

"Ha. In one piece?" I shifted my feet and jumped from the boat.

Nooky had stayed utterly quiet; now she leapt onto shore and immediately starting sniffing. As she caught the hot scent of a moose, she gave a deep-throated growl and flattened her ears against her head.

We tied the boat, stumbling in our eagerness to get going. Clipping a leash onto Nooky's collar, I said, "Should we make noise to let the moose know we're here?"

"Good idea," Dick said.

"Okay!" We began trudging across the muddy and rock-filled portage path.

"How are we doing?" I yelled.

"Great!" Dick called back.

I followed him, tugging Nooky, whose eyes were darting from side to side. Then she balked. "Oh, come on girl," I wheedled. "Don't dig in your heels. We have to hurry." Her ears stayed flattened. She might have run off if she hadn't been leashed.

I felt jittery. My heart lurched at every sound. A bird fluttering in the underbrush sent my blood racing. Was that a branch cracking? I halted and listened. Nothing.

Normally, the walk across the portage was a brief and inconvenient part of a getting to or from the Gunflint Trail—something I hardly even thought about. Today, it felt like hours instead of the ten minutes it actually took.

We finally reached the other side of the portage's narrow strip of land, and Dick yanked the canoe from its hiding spot in the underbrush. Nooky, who usually loved to sniff and explore, leaped directly into the canoe and sat there with set ears that pled, "Let's get out of here."

We did.

Fifteen minutes later, we pulled up to the front of our cabin. As we landed and I held the canoe fast to our small homemade log dock, I realized I wasn't homesick any more. The sad feeling had completely vanished. I jumped from the canoe and headed up to the cabin, happy to be home.

8

ONE WITH NATURE?

One morning over coffee I mused, "I'm really getting in shape. I could hike circles around my city self."

"I wouldn't exactly say that." Dick gave me a skeptical look and then dodged my playful punch.

I was definitely more relaxed. After three weeks of wilderness life, my shoulders had loosened, my teeth had stopped grinding, and I felt much calmer than the young woman who'd hopped from the canoe to find a broken cabin window the night we'd arrived.

Rain had been falling for several days and wind battered at the windows. I'd just returned from our hole-in-the-ground biffy, exhilarated by the contrast of the cold wet outdoors and the warm cozy cabin. "It's good to depend on no one but ourselves. I think we're getting damn good at handling this wilderness stuff. "

Dick nodded and poured himself another cup of coffee. I leaned back, gave a lazy stretch, and watched rain streak down the front window while we discussed daily chores. No need to hurry this morning.

But that night a strange sound woke me from a sound sleep.

Tap…tap…tap…I nudged Dick. "There's a noise." What could it be? Someone at the door? Who could be tromping around at this time of night? Maybe a family emergency?

Dick pulled himself out of bed, grabbed his flashlight and beamed its yellow light around the cabin walls. He quickly traced the sound to the broken back window where a plastic tarp still served as a glass pane. We'd been meaning to fix it, but cutting firewood had taken precedence. "It's some kind of moisture," he said and peered closer at the window. "It's snow! Heavy wet snow!"

"But it's only the first week in October," I said. "Isn't this too early? The locals all say mid-October."

"Doesn't matter what they say." Dick walked to the front door. "It's snowing out there. I'm taking a leak," and he headed out into a swirl of snow.

"Wait for me. I have to go too," I yelled and scrambled out of bed to join him. Outside, big wet snowflakes were gently settling over the dark woods. We stepped off the deck and wandered off in different directions into the underbrush. The next morning, convinced that winter was now just around the corner, we got started on a project we'd postponed more than once: to scout out an overland path from our cabin to the Gunflint Trail. It was an absolute necessity.

During freeze-up, when ice formed on Tucker and Little Iron Lakes, the canoe would be useless, and we'd be forced to walk through the woods to the Gunflint Trail. It would be our only connection with civilization. Once the ice got thick enough, we'd be able to skim across it on a snowmobile, but during the interim, we'd have to hoof it. That meant walking a third of a mile to the Tucker River, then another three quarters of a mile to the Gunflint Trail. We'd have to hike hills, valleys, woods, and cross the river, which thankfully was running at an autumnal low.

By the time we finished our coffee and stepped outside, the day was warming and the previous night's snow was melting, dropping from pine boughs in clumps, vanishing from old brown fern leaves, and dripping from twigs. But it had done its job. It had jolted us into action.

The goal we'd set for the first day was to break and blaze a trail as far as the spruce swamp that lay between us and the Tucker River. Past that swamp lay a high ridge that flattened eastward toward a narrow section of the Tucker River where we could easily cross. Once across the river, another three quarters of a mile of wilderness had to be marked and blazed before we reached the Gunflint Trail. But for today, we simply needed to clear the segment between the cabin and the swamp.

I was in high spirits as we headed for the swamp. Each of us had a job to do. Dick had been to the spruce swamp numerous times, and the makeshift trail he'd used was still visible. Today, he would further define the path with blaze marks and use the chainsaw to cut up saplings and other debris that had fallen across the path. I would follow behind to pick up the debris and throw it in the woods.

Nooky ran circles around us, yet never strayed far.

I was eager to see the spruce swamp. Dick had cut firewood back here and often talked about its strangeness. "You have to see it to understand," he'd said. "It's hard to describe."

I thought about that as we worked together to open a broader and more well-defined path through the moose maple and hazel shrubs. Then Dick stopped and pointed to a stand of tall tree trunks looming ahead. "There it is."

We moved closer, and I saw he was right. There was something unique about these surroundings. In the absence of chainsaw chatter, a hush filled the air as we neared the towering canopy of dark trunks. The spruce swamp. I took a deep breath. The atmosphere rising from the boggy floor of lush, rock-covered green moss felt magical and mystical.

As we skirted the center of the bog, staying on drier ground, Dick pointed to a large dry hummock showed an indentation left by a bedding moose or deer. He pointed to the remnants of last summer's pitcher plants—carnivorous plants whose pitcher-shaped leaves lured and trapped insects. Then ate them.

I noted abundant patches of Labrador tea plants. A Gunflint Trail neighbor had pointed out this unusual plant that survives cold, heat, drought, and floods and suggested we brew its leaves into a tea. I stripped a few handfuls of the narrow leathery leaves and tucked them in my backpack pocket. "I'll make tea tonight," I said.

"Let's keep moving." We forged ahead and had almost passed the swamp's end when a ruffed grouse burst up from the roots of a fallen spruce. All three of us jumped, and Nooky growled, but the bird flew to a nearby spruce bough for cover, and we let it be.

"We'll go as far as the Tucker River today," Dick said, "then finish the rest another day." Before long we broke from the woods and found ourselves at the top of a ridge. We could see the Tucker River below us, shallow and slow-running in its autumn mode but sparkling in the sun. This signaled the end of today's adventure.

As the sun passed its zenith, we turned and began trudging home. When we entered the spruce swamp, we passed the giant fallen spruce, and once again, the ruffed grouse flew up and into cover.

"Next time, we'll bring a lunch and work all day to finish the rest of the path," Dick said as the roof of the cabin appeared in the distance. I agreed. The serious work of clearing a trail would begin on another day. No reason to panic. It would be quite a while before the lakes froze up.

9

THE FRESH HERRING

The next morning we made our biweekly trek to the mailbox on the Gunflint Trail. I loved getting letters from home, and every week, at least one personal letter arrived. As the canoe skimmed across the watery three miles to the portage, I wondered how much mail we'd receive today.

Dick had installed a mailbox next to the box for Loon Lake Lodge, and although our mail frequently sat for several days before we picked it up, nothing was ever missing, nor was our mailbox vandalized. But no letters awaited us today, and we trekked down the long driveway to visit our nearest neighbors at Loon Lake Lodge, the Johnson brothers, Willard and Kermit, and their father.

The two brothers were lanky outdoorsmen who owned and operated the resort and always welcomed visitors with a cup of coffee. Their white-haired father, eighty-five-year-old Henning, loved to tell stories of his Swedish childhood in Duluth at the turn of the twentieth century.

After a chatting session and several cups of strong coffee, we began the usual good-bye ritual. I grabbed our jackets, which were hanging on a hook by the door.

"Stay for dinner," Kermit suggested. "We've got fresh herring."

I'd never eaten fresh herring, but it was locally considered a delicacy, and at this time of year the little fish were abundant and easily netted.

"No. Thank you much, but it's getting too late." I turned to gauge Dick's response. His face told me he also wanted to get home. "I don't want to cross the portage in the dark."

Will responded with the neighborliness common to Gunflint Trail residents. "Well then, we'll wrap up a couple of fillets for you. Fix 'em when you get home." Henning, who was already in the kitchen, wasted no time rewrapping two plump fillets in white butcher paper and within minutes handed over a neat packet of fresh herring for our dinner. I was thrilled.

One dreary aspect of life in the woods was a lack of fresh food. Without refrigeration, our menus were limited, and the weather was still too warm to store perishables. Occasionally Dick shot a partridge, and we feasted on its succulent white meat; and sometimes we'd catch a walleye or two, but most of our meals were bland canned stuff. Fresh fish sounded wonderful.

As our little boat chugged across Little Iron, I thought about dinner. When we crossed the portage and got into the canoe, I was dreaming about crispy fried fish. As I pushed the canoe away from the portage and Dick started the four-horsepower motor, fresh fish was still on my mind. A straggly alder branch grabbed at my hat, but I barely noticed. In half an hour I would be pan-frying the lovely pink herring pieces. And as our canoe passed the familiar rocks and trees of the shoreline, I dreamed of crusty golden herring fillets. I could almost taste them.

The sun was low in a red sky as we landed at our log dock. "Go fry the fish," Dick suggested. "I'll take care of everything else."

I loped up the hill and hurried into the cabin, where I slung off my backpack, lifted the flap, and reached inside for the white paper packet.

Not there. This was impossible. *The fish had to be there. Where else would they be?* I scrambled deeper inside the pack, my heart sinking as I scattered items on the cabin floor. Panic flooded my thoughts. Several used Kleenexes floated down, but nothing resembling a white packet. A red bandana, but nothing under it. My billfold lay snugly on the bottom of the pack, but no herring fillets. There was no sign of the fish package.

I ran to the door, cranked it open, and called in a shrill voice. "Dick!" He was still tying the canoe to the dock. He looked up. "Is the white package in the canoe?" I crossed my fingers. The herring fillets had to be there. They just had to be. "They aren't in my backpack," I added.

"I don't think so." Dick pulled his flashlight from a pocket and searched the canoe bottom. He lifted paddles and ropes. "Nothing," he reported. "Maybe they dropped out of your pack!" "Nothing here." He picked up his fanny pack and slowly walked up the hill. "I'll check along our path." He stooped over every bush and rock outcropping as he walked.

"Nothing," he reported again, entering the cabin.

"I can't believe it," I wailed. "I lost the herring!"

"Look harder," Dick suggested. We searched everything again, though in my heart of hearts, I knew the fish weren't there. We rummaged through coat pockets. No herring. The canoe. The backpack. My jacket pocket. Dick's jacket pocket. The herring fillets weren't with us. I had dropped them somewhere along the way home.

"What's the alternative meal?" Dick looked glum. The sun had set and darkness had set in.

"Creamed dried beef on toast," I answered morosely. He didn't even look at me. Chipped creamed beef was his least favorite meal.

I melted a glob of butter, added flour, and stirred in canned milk. Opening a jar of dried beef, I cut it into small pieces and added them to the sauce. The final step was to toast two bread slices over the Coleman stove burner. When all was finished I handed Dick his meal with a sigh.

I took a bite. Bland and salty. We could be eating fresh, crisply fried herring strips.

After a silent dinner, Dick cleared his throat and made a proposition. "There's one hope," he said as I cleared the remnants of toast and creamed beef. "If tonight is cold enough, and no animals find the fillets, we might have a chance of retrieving them tomorrow."

I tried to sound upbeat. "Do you think?"

"They have to be somewhere between the car and home."

"Let's give it a try."

As we prepped for bed, I tried not to be overly optimistic, but I couldn't help myself. We simply had to find those fillets.

The ground was white with frost the next morning. We putt-putted down the lake in the canoe feeling cautiously optimistic, and landed at the portage.

I crossed my fingers as we slowly walked over the muddy, rock-strewn path looking for a white packet in the thick underbrush. We reached the other side empty-handed.

We got into the boat and, shivering in the cool morning, crossed Little Iron, then retraced our steps from the landing to the Bronco parked on the Gunflint Trail.

I had given up hope. With slumping shoulders, I approached our vehicle. This was my last chance. Dejected thoughts filled my mind as I reached for the passenger door handle and looked down.

There it was! The white packet of fillets lay on the ground, under my car door, where it had dropped from the Duluth pack. A miracle! Grabbing it, I shrieked. "They're here! I found them!"

Dick ran to my side. As I tore open the packet, I noted little holes in the paper.

"Mice." Dick commented as the fillets came to light.

"But look!" My voice shook with excitement. "They chewed the paper, but the fish is fine."

"Not a single mouse bite," Dick commented. "How lucky are we?"

Feeling jubilant, we returned to the cabin and burst through the door. I unwrapped the fillets, rolled them in flour, and fried them to a crisp. Wasting no time, we ate immediately and called it brunch.

It was wonderful.

10

Freeze-Up

It was mail day. I slipped into my quilted corduroy winter jacket, pulled a warm wool hat over my head, and headed through the blustery morning to the canoe where Dick and Nooky waited.

Fast-moving clouds scuttled across the bright blue sky, and the bare birch and poplar tree branches rattled, but we wouldn't dream of letting a little thing like wind or cold stop us from picking up the mail. Setting my backpack on the floor of the canoe, I hopped in and opened its flap, making sure the two letters I'd placed inside were still there. One was to my parents, the other to my sister.

Dick started the motor and we putt-putted slowly down the length of Tucker Lake. Although the bright yellow and rich gold of birch and poplar leaves had been replaced by stark brown, the deep green of pine and spruce lightened the drabness of the otherwise denuded forest. Shivering, I pulled my jacket's collar tighter around my neck and made a mental note to buy a warm neck wrap next time we went to town.

As we neared the eastern end of Tucker, something in the atmosphere changed; a frigid heaviness filled the air, and I braced against the biting cold. Good thing we were almost at the portage. I was eager to start moving around again and warm myself up.

Without warning, the canoe stopped dead in the water. Startled, I turned to Dick. He looked confused as he returned my questioning look. The engine was still running, aimlessly churning the water behind the canoe. We both gazed down at the lake's surface, which suddenly looked unfamiliar. It was shiny. It was flat. I reached out and touched it.

It was ice.

Dumbfounded, we stared at this phenomena for a few moments in silence. Then I said: "Shall we go back?"

Dick looked puzzled. "Don't know." We thought some more. What should we do?

Finally, Dick turned off the motor, grabbed one of the canoe paddles, raised it over his head, and brought it down with a huge *thwack*! The ice shattered. "It's not as thick as I thought." He handed me the other paddle. "Let's try chopping our way to shore."

Lifting the other paddle, I whacked it down. The ice tinkled as it shattered, and I breathed a sigh of relief. Within minutes, by first whacking, then paddling, then whacking again, we had almost reached the portage landing. I felt cocky.

"Where there's a will, there's a way." I gave the last bit of ice another wicked thwack and looked back at the lake where a narrow path of dark water and white broken ice followed us to shore. The canoe touched land, and I stepped out to hold it steady for Dick.

But Dick worried as he climbed out. "Little Iron is a lot shallower than Tucker. It could be frozen over."

We hid the canoe behind a thicket as we always did and scrambled over the rocky path to the other end of the portage.

Dick had been right. I could see the flat ice of Little Iron's shoreline stretching far out into the main part of the lake. Dick picked up a sturdy stick and thumped it down on the ice. The ice held firm. Too thick for us to break.

No chance we would be crossing Little Iron in the boat.

"We have a choice." Dick said. "Shall we turn around and take the canoe home or walk through the woods? The Gunflint Trail is north. We go straight north and hit it."

Nothing would stop me from checking my mail. "Let's walk." I said. "We might get mail."

Dick took out his compass, we shrugged into our backpacks, and into the woods we trekked, heading north.

I was elated. Another challenge had presented itself, and we were dealing with it. The hiking itself was exciting. Large windfalls that probably had never been seen by human eyes frequently blocked our progress. These masses of fallen trees, dead branches, and moss-covered logs, piled up helter-skelter, fascinated me. But skirting these windfalls made for a winding, looping, exhausting path. Just "heading north" wasn't as easy as it sounded.

At one point, as we faced yet another insurmountable pile of windfall, I secretly cursed it. *Looks like rubble.* I longed for a smooth road, a sidewalk, a gravel path—anything but the thick forest through which we were thrashing. Then we met up with a stand of spruce trees whose boughs swept the forest floor, forcing us to detour once again. I would have given anything to be rid of the heavy jacket I was wearing. It had felt cozy and warm while shivering in the canoe. Now it weighed on my shoulders like a sand-filled Santa bag.

Dick trudged ahead as we circled the spruce stand, occasionally stopping to check his compass. *What a great form of exercise*, I thought grimly as I stopped to wipe the sweat off my forehead, then double-timed it to keep up with Dick. Even Nooky's tongue was lolling.

After what seemed an unending succession of windfalls, gullies, hills, and tree branches whipping me in the face, I finally caught a glimpse of a cleared area ahead. As we broke through a fringe of underbrush onto gravel, Dick said, "We're at the old logging road. Just an easy walk to the Trail now."

Thank heavens. I'd been about to lose faith in his navigational skills. We'd hiked only a mile, but what a mile! It had taken over an hour to traverse, and I gulped at the realization that we'd have to return the same way.

At least our perseverance was rewarded with several letters from home. I set my two letters in the mailbox and lifted the small flag to notify the postman there was mail to be picked up, but as we started back home, at the spot where we'd come out on the Gunflint Trail I sighed. *I suppose I'd better get used to hiking.* With heavy legs, we retraced our windfall-filled steps back to the portage.

Halfway through the return ordeal, Dick remarked, "We'll have to finish the path behind our cabin fast and make sure that route is easier than this one."

I agreed.

ఞ

For the next few days, we worked at a feverish pace. Starting where we had left off at the spruce swamp, we marked and cleared a path leading to the Tucker River. Five or six inches of snow covered the ground, and the work was exhausting. I often felt sweaty, yet the work also filled me with a feeling of satisfaction. We were doing something worthwhile.

We took a short rest at noon while Dick made a small campfire and brewed coffee, then we sat on a log and ate the peanut butter sandwiches I'd packed.

As I munched, my eyes swept up and down the river. It was narrow and slow-moving, with yellow reeds growing along at its shores. A single bluebill duck rounded the bend and swam towards us, finally taking flight.

"Time to move on," Dick announced. Shivering from the

cold, I agreed. Cramming the wax paper and empty brown lunch bag into my backpack, I stood up and followed.

The river was at an autumnal low, and we easily crossed at a narrow, rock-strewn spot. We moved north as Dick cut up old logs and tree branches with his chainsaw and I came behind him picking up debris and clearing the trail. We stopped often to consider alternative directions, hoping to make the route as easy as possible, but often we had no choice but to blaze a circuitous path around a hill or declivity, and we were also forced to add distance as we circumnavigated windfalls and tree clumps. Keeping to a straight line in the thick and undulating woods was not really an option.

I felt a surge of pride when we finally walked the last one hundred feet through the woods and broke out to the black asphalt of the Trail. "Whoo hoo!" I shouted. "We have a walking path to the Trail!"

We returned to the cabin along our new thoroughfare, blazing a few trees for good measure, and felt very satisfied with what we'd accomplished.

෴

The next morning, a new set of realities presented themselves: "Dick, we're running out of clean clothes." I dug around in the laundry bag looking for a pair of not too dirty socks. "And we're running out of groceries. I think we'd better go to town."

With one backpack full of dirty clothes and one empty, we hiked down our newly blazed path with newfound exuberance. The walk was pleasant, almost easy, unlike the high-intensity pace of the previous day, when there had been lots of work to do. And the forty-mile drive to Grand Marais was a breeze.

Once we reached town, we followed the pattern we'd developed over the past few weeks. Dick dropped me at the laundromat and I did the wash while he ran his errands. During the wash cycle, I strolled around the corner to Leng's Fountain. I treated myself to a chocolate ice cream cone, purchased at its fabulous old-fashioned counter. I also bought an array of magazines, *Vogue* among them. (I didn't want to lose track of fashion.)

When the last piece of laundry was dried, Dick helped load it into a Duluth pack, and we ate chili at the El Ray Café. Making one final stop at Matt Johnson's old grocery store, we bought a two-week supply of food—canned tuna, flour, tortillas, canned soups, saltines—and then headed back up the Gunflint Trail, sated with city life.

When we reached our new path it was 2:30, but the sun was low—darkness was setting in earlier every day—and we wasted little time filling the Duluth packs with groceries and laundry. I hoisted a pack to my shoulders, feeling jaunty—heck, I was in the best shape of my life—and was surprised when my knees buckled. I blinked. "Dick," I was a bit testy. "Why did you give me the heavier pack?"

"I didn't." He pulled his pack onto his shoulders.

"Oh." I was flummoxed. If this was the lighter of the two packs, I would hate to lift the heavier one. I'd carried weighty backpacks before but nothing like this, and I had to carry this burden on my back all the way home before dark. I had no choice.

As we started down our new path I stayed quiet, saving my breath. Every ounce of strength was sucked away by the simple act of moving forward. No time or energy to be wasted. We trudged in silence over hills, down ridges, around spruce swamps. It seemed that no sooner had we climbed one hill, another rose to greet us, and I groaned silently each time I spotted a rise in the ground. Dick wasn't as lively as usual, but he moved faster than I. I straggled but kept moving.

Time seemed to stop; the walk seemed endless. My back ached and the backpack straps dug into my shoulders with a painful bite.

As we skirted a stand of spruce trees, Dick turned. "How're you doing?" He looked concerned.

"Fine," I lied. "I might be a little slow, but I'm coming." Since this single brief remark took away my breath, I went silent, but thoughts flew through my head. This was awful, the worst pain I'd ever felt. I wanted to drop to the ground and cry. But that wouldn't help. Desperately I searched my mind for a way to make things better. What was best way to get through this grueling experience? How could I take my mind away from the pain the shoulder straps were inflicting on me? I had no answer.

Then I suddenly remembered a trick I used once or twice at the dentist office. While the drill shrieked its high pitch screech and the smell of burned enamel filled the air, visualizing favorite foods or beautiful places had helped me get through the nastiness.

I'll try that. Picturing a box full of luscious chocolate-covered cherries, I focused on the smell, the smooth texture of the filling, and the rich taste. The pain in my shoulders and back seemed to decrease. *This might just work.* Next, I imagined sniffing a vase of gorgeous lavender and purple orchids; the sweet fragrance took my mind from my discomfort. *Don't stop now.* Now, I imagined lounging on a tropical beach watching a beautiful sunrise, with warm air caressing my face and the sound of ocean waves lapping.

Again Dick called back, "You okay?"

I wasn't, but felt slightly better. "I'm doing okay." A fantasy wedge of apple pie à la mode was helping to take my mind off the discomfort.

But Dick wasn't completely fooled. "We'll stop at the river and rest," he said and continued his sturdy steps forward. I trudged behind.

It felt like forever, but only twenty minutes had passed when we glimpsed the gleaming water of the Tucker River below us. Dick took confident strides; I stumbled down the sharp grade. "Careful," he warned. "Don't go too fast. You'll fall."

Tears of joy filled my eyes at the sight of this halfway point, and I carelessly increased my speed forward. Gravity took over and my knees buckled. *Slow down. You made it this far. Don't be an idiot and hurt yourself.* Although every nerve in my body told me to run so I could throw off my pack and rest along the flat river bottom, I crept at a snail's pace. Finally, I reached it.

At the river's edge, a hard truth hit. Sitting down was not an option. If I sat down I wouldn't have the strength to rise again. But there must be some way I could rest. I looked at a small birch tree and had an idea. Backing against it might just take off some of the pressure. Lowering my knees slightly, I took several backward steps, and leaned my backpack against the white trunk. It worked! What a relief.

Dick, on the other hand, slid his arms from his backpack straps, set it on the ground, looked at me, and commented, "Take it off. It'll feel better."

"No. I'll play it safe." I leaned my back with its load against the tree. It wasn't total but even a smallest respite felt wonderful.

The second half of the walk was no better than the first. Along with visualizing, I repeated hopeful mantras: As we headed uphill from the river and moved towards the spruce swamp, I repeated, "It's the home stretch...almost there...home stretch...almost there." I trudged, visualizing our tiny cabin and its beautiful entryway.

Finally, when I felt unable to take another step, I spotted the cabin roof in the deepening twilight through the trees. "Almost home," I repeated, "almost home." Stumbling over the last two hundred feet with unbelievably heavy legs, I climbed the cabin steps and clumsily pushed open the door.

I staggered across the room and dropped on the bunk bed like an overturned turtle. The stark plywood walls looked welcoming. Though the fireplace was cold, soon it would crackle with warm yellow flames. I was home. The horrendous hike was over.

But it wasn't over for good. We hiked that same path for the next few weeks until the lake ice was safe. I never again filled a pack as full as I had for that first overland trek.

Mother Nature had taught me another lesson. Watch the size of your purchases if you're going to carry them on your back.

11

Pre-Winter

The days moved quickly until Halloween lurked around the corner. I realized with a pang that for the first time in my life I wouldn't be wearing a costume or passing out candy, not to mention attending Halloween parties.

To satisfy my inner child, I bought a small pumpkin in Grand Marais, carved a jack-o-lantern, placed a candle inside the orange globe, and set it on a stump behind the cabin on Halloween night. Its orange face grinned eerily against a background of silvery birch trunks and leafless underbrush.

Dick smiled when I pointed it out to Nooky, but her twitching nose drew her interest to a windborne scent, and she scampered around the cabin to investigate. The candle burned out, and the evil looking slit eyes of my jack-o-lantern disappeared. That was it—the full extent of my celebration. There was nothing left but go to bed.

The next morning, the sight of my forlorn pumpkin resting on a tree stump gave me an idea. This was potential food. I'd never known anyone to make pumpkin pie from an actual pumpkin, but why not? I didn't have whipped cream, but heck, a pie would taste good anyway.

Baking pie would brighten the gloomy atmosphere in the cabin on this drizzly November 1. With a cold wind spattering raindrops against the cabin windows, and the sound of Dick's chainsaw echoing faintly through the trees as it did every morning when he cut firewood, I began cutting the orange sphere into small pieces and dreamed of spicy, fragrant pie slices.

Several problems presented themselves immediately. For one thing, the pumpkin shell was much thicker and tougher than I'd anticipated. Although Dick always kept my kitchen knives razor sharp, my first downward plunge with the knife bounced off the orange shell. This wasn't going to be easy. I stubbornly hacked and finally opened up a wedge, then kept cutting until the pieces were small enough to fit in my kettle.

The second problem emerged only gradually, as I noticed that although the pumpkin pieces had been immersed in simmering water for almost an hour, they stubbornly refused to soften. I labored my Coleman stove to its limit keeping the water at a boil. Would this really work, I wondered? When Dick came in for lunch, soaking wet and hungry, he glanced skeptically at the simmering pot.

"Pumpkin pie," I answered his questioning look. "Hopefully we'll have it for dessert tonight—if it turns out." He hastily spooned down a bowl of vegetable beef soup and returned to the damp, chilly forest for more woodcutting, and I returned to my cooking project.

While Nooky slept at the front door, I threw several extra logs in the Franklin wood stove to achieve a good baking temperature, then rolled out a piecrust. The pumpkin pieces had finally gotten tender, so I mashed them, added an egg and then a goodly amount of brown sugar, figuring sugar never hurt. A sprinkle of ginger, some cinnamon, and (after a quick search through my small cupboard) a pinch of nutmeg. A moment of sheer panic struck when I remembered that custard pie required milk, but I scrounged through the pantry shelves and unearthed a can of evaporated milk. I stirred the conglomeration vigorously and finally poured the gooey mixture into the piecrust.

Standing back to survey my almost-finished project, I felt a tingle of pride, while simultaneously wondering if the experiment would actually turn out.

I tucked the pie in my Dutch oven, set it on the iron grate inside the stove over glowing red embers, and closed the doors.

Soon the cabin was filled with a fragrant, spicy aroma. A half hour later, I pulled the Dutch oven away from the heat and lifted the lid apprehensively, I was greeting with the sight of a smooth, creamy-looking pumpkin filling surrounded by a lightly browned crust.

My pumpkin pie experiment was a success.

We enjoyed big wedges of pumpkin pie that night, delicious even without whipped cream. It was the best pumpkin pie I ever made.

Feeling cocky about my cooking accomplishment, in the following week's letters to home I told everyone: "I made the best pumpkin pie in the world."

But my command of Dutch oven pumpkin pie was short-lived. I've never been able to duplicate that marvelous creation, though lord knows I've tried. Maybe the wood stove created a better flavor. Maybe I was more patient while living in the woods and baked it longer. Maybe we were hungrier. Whatever the reason, to this day not a single pumpkin pie I've baked has surpassed the one on Tucker Lake.

❧

Several days later, the dreary November weather disappeared. Temperatures soared, clouds vanished, and we were blessed with a glorious Second Summer, blue sky and all. The ice on Tucker Lake was still unsafe, so we resigned ourselves to hiking our overland path when we wanted or needed civilization.

Now that the tourist season was over, Gunflint Trail residents had free time on their hands once again and were more gregarious. Resorts had closed or reduced their hours, giving owners and fishing guides time to socialize. On our biweekly hikes to the Trail for mail, we always stopped at Loon Lake Lodge to say hello and met other Trail residents who also dropped in.

The Loon Lake Lodge people always insisted we stay for a meal, and we often did. They were happy to share not only food but recipes, and many years later, I still use the lasagna, potato soup, and scalloped potatoes recipes they gave me.

We enjoyed the company, though it always felt good to get back to our cozy little cabin.

≈

One morning as I finished sweeping the floor, I opened the door to empty the dustpan and was shocked to see a strange man on my doorstep. His dark form loomed in the doorframe, and the sinister smile on his face sent chills down my spine.

Where was the shotgun? And how far was Dick down the lakeshore? Panicky thoughts flashed through my mind.

Then I recognized him. It was Al, a fishing guide we'd met the previous day at Loon Lake Lodge.

I pulled myself together. What was the matter with me? He wasn't a big man, and I'd misjudged his smile. It was awkward and shy, not sinister. I'd let my imagination run wild.

Struggling to replace my shocked demeanor with a friendly smile, I greeted him. "Hi, Al."

"Just stopped to say hello." His large hand pushed forward as he handed me a Taystee bread bag filled with Polish sausage and garden potatoes, carrots, and apples.

"Thank you," I said. "Come in. Dick's down the shore, cutting wood."

He must have realized he'd given me a jolt and perhaps felt

uncomfortable being alone in the cabin without Dick. "I'll go find him," he said quickly. Adjusting the front of his grimy blue tanker jacket under which a tiny Chihuahua nestled, he turned and trotted in the direction of Dick's screeching chainsaw.

I shut the door and looked at the food he'd thrust in my hands. In the tradition of Gunflint Trail people, I understood that I was expected to offer coffee to company, especially someone who'd just hiked a mile and a half through the woods. In this case, since he'd brought food, it was only proper that I cook it.

I counted the potatoes and carrots. Plenty. Along with a batch of homemade rolls rising near the stove, the Polish sausage and veggies would make a nice little meal. I set to work cooking.

That was the first of many visits from Al. He was a rough-hewn and solitary but gentle man who loved dogs and harbored a strong distrust of the human race, especially politicians. He spoke only once of horrific experiences in World War II's Battle of the Bulge and never said another word about them. He refused to vote in any election, claiming it didn't matter how a person voted. Politicians were all the same.

Midafternoon, I served an early supper. I didn't realize, as I passed out tin plates filled with polish sausage, carrots, and potatoes, that Al was to become a frequent visitor that November and throughout the next year. He always walked through the woods, even in summer when he could have used a canoe or boat. He always brought gifts, and he introduced us to much wilderness lore. Along with his garden produce he brought teas and showed us how to make them; red rose tea flavored with home-dried orange rinds and Labrador tea spiced with peppermint or cloves. I always enjoyed his gifts and shared knowledge. However, the day came when, finally, one of his gifts tested my self-image.

It was a bright, brisk November morning. Second Summer was fading and temperatures were falling. Al had tramped through the woods again. His visits were becoming so common,

I didn't even lift an eyebrow when his dark figure burst from the woods.

Once inside the cabin he held out another Taystee Bread bag, something he always did. "Here's a little something for you." He said. I accepted the bag, looked more closely and almost dropped it. This time, instead of carrots or potatoes, there was something raw and bloody inside.

"Thank you." I tried not to look repulsed as my fingertips tentatively accepted the gory gift.

"It's a beaver leg." His round face beamed with pride. "Tasty and good food too. You young people are always talking about organic and natural, and that"—he pointed at the bag I was gingerly holding—"that beaver meat is pure. No preservatives or chemicals there."

"Really nice of you, Al," I blurted with phony enthusiasm. The very idea of chewing and swallowing beaver meat made my stomach churn. (Heck, I didn't even like venison.) But I couldn't let Al know. "How do I fix it?" I hoped my voice sounded gracious.

He hadn't noticed my apprehension and warmed to this topic. His round face broke into a huge smile. "The main thing," he instructed, his eyes glowing with the pride of an expert, "is to cut off all the fat. I've already taken off the scent glands, but you need to get rid of any fat. Then you can prepare it like beef."

He sat down to wait for the cup of coffee I always offered. "And don't worry about fixing it while I'm here. I can't stay today. Dogs are home alone, and my fire will go out if I don't get back soon."

Dick joined us, his cheeks ruddy from the cold, and after coffee and a plate of my homemade chocolate chip cookies, Al bade us farewell and trudged back into the woods.

Twenty-four hours passed before I found the courage to face the beaver leg. Cooking a rodent was not an appealing task. Finally, late the following afternoon, I forced myself into action. The bloody lump of meat had to be dealt with, though I dreaded it. Easing into the task, I first asked Dick, "Could you please cut off all the fat?" The thought of touching the bloody mess gave me the creeps.

Dick took out his sharpest knife and set the hunk of meat on the cutting board, where it rested like a large, deviant turkey drumstick. Without the slightest qualm, he whittled white globules away from the red flesh. I watched, fascinated.

He was doing so well I let him continue without interruption and busied myself pouring a cup of flour and a pinch of salt and pepper into a plastic bag. Maybe I could avoid touching the rodent meat.

"Would you mind cutting it into small pieces?" I asked when he finished carving out the fat. "As long as your hands are already gunky?"

He obliged, and as he went to work again I heated some cooking oil a cast-iron frying pan. So far I hadn't had to touch the raw meat, thank goodness. I took a breath of silent relief.

But I wasn't fooling anybody. Dick knew my dislike of gamey meat, so when he finished cubing it, he said, "Don't worry. I'll drop it into the flour. It's obvious you don't want to touch it."

My only answer was a sheepish grin.

When all the red meat chunks were covered with flour, I opened the bag and let the floured meat drop into the sizzling fat.

At this point, it was easy to move the meat bits around with a fork until they turned crispy brown. During that time I had a chance to get used to the strange meat. I took a closer look. It looked like beef. I leaned down and sniffed. It didn't smell unusual. Al had been right. Without the fat, beaver flesh closely resembled beef.

However, it was wild meat and needed to be well cooked. Rare beaver meat might not be safe. I sautéed the beaver chunks far past a reasonable time.

Finally, when I was totally satisfied the meat was well-done,

I set the cooked beaver on a nice platter. "Our first meal of beaver leg," I announced, plunking the down the plate. "Ta-da"!

Dick took the first bite. He chewed laboriously as I anxiously watched. After swallowing, he took a long drink of water. "Not bad."

I took a mouthful. A pleasant meaty flavor hit my tongue. I chewed and chewed and chewed. It was good, but tough. Much too tough. In my zeal not to undercook, I'd overcooked. However, it *was* food, and we were hungry. We chewed and chewed and chewed until all the meat was gone.

With our first beaver meal under our belts, we went on to have many more. Al brought beaver meat numerous times during the next year. I swallowed my fastidiousness and learned to cut fat from the bloody hunks, even losing my horror of its touch. I became proud of my ability to cube the meat and roll it in flour. I learned to slowly simmer it in a stew until the meat was tenderized and delicious.

Beaver stew became a regular part of our menu, but I was always grateful that Al continued to cut off the scent glands.

ॐ

One morning we woke to -10° F with two inches of newly fallen snow on the ground. The frigid temperatures and white ground cover sent us scurrying to finish winterizing our lives. Dick insulated and covered the inside cabin walls with plywood sheets. When he wasn't doing that, he maniacally cut firewood, fearing we wouldn't have enough.

I kept up his energy levels with huge breakfasts of bacon, eggs, and toast and even bigger evening meals, always with desserts of homemade pies, cookies, or brownies.

One evening, after a chaotically busy day—I'd baked a large batch of sourdough bread while Dick split and stacked a huge pile of firewood—we stepped into our snowshoes and took an after-dinner walk on the path behind the cabin.

The brightness of the moon and the whiteness of the snow rendered our flashlights unnecessary. Stars glittered high in the black sky, and as we stood awed by the beauty, a small animal scuttled through the brush. In the distance, the kerosene lantern lights glowed a warm yellow in our cabin windows. The moment took my breath away. *We should do this more often*, I thought.

Mostly, we spent our evenings inside, listening to the radio. Dick's father had given us an old radio that we hooked up to an antenna wire strung between two trees. In the evenings, we listened to WGN, a Chicago station, smugly chuckling at reports of horrific traffic jams, but we enjoying the chatter and information just the same.

With our lives humming smoothly, I was unprepared one night when, without warning, cabin fever struck. We'd lived in the wilderness for two months. We sat, as always, with legs propped up near the wood fire. I was reading a book and Dick was fiddling with the radio. He tuned in the *Dan Price Call-In Show*. That night's topic featured wines, food, and Chicago's best restaurants.

As we listened to descriptions of Beaujolais and Pouilly-Fuissé wine and tantalizing dinners of chicken Kiev, I was overwhelmed by a fierce longing to put on fancy clothes and go to a nice restaurant, complete with white linen tablecloths and a snooty maître d'.

Where did that come from? I thought. I love it in the woods. And yet…"Wouldn't it be fun to go out on the town tonight? Have some good wine?" I was thinking of bars and restaurants we had frequented in Minneapolis.

Dick caught the mood. He swept me into his arms and waltzed me around the cabin while Nooky watched, slightly bewildered. "Someday," he promised, "we'll have a horribly expensive fully stocked wine cellar in our basement."

We whirled around the cabin, circling feverishly until I crumpled, laughing. "We're getting goofy." I still felt restless. "What's wrong with us?"

"Cabin fever?" Dick asked.

"I think it is." I was perplexed. This was the first time I'd felt bored by our cabin life.

We left for Minneapolis two days later, eager to see everyone and celebrate Thanksgiving with our families.

12

What Are We Made Of?

One week later, the Thanksgiving trip to Minneapolis was over. As Dick pulled our vehicle off the Gunflint Trail onto the logging road where our footpath to the cabin began, I breathed a big sigh of relief. We'd been gone only seven days, but I'd had enough of city life. No more cabin fever for me.

He turned off the ignition and jumped from the vehicle, trudging through snow to retrieve our Sno-Pony snowmobile from its hiding place in a thicket. The winter sun was bright and the blue sky cloudless, but we knew daylight was half gone on this first of December.

No time for dawdling.

As we quickly loaded a carful of gear and food supplies onto the sled, I thought back over the gatherings of the past week. Family and friends had all asked the same question. When are you coming back?

I had often answered the question with a light-hearted and dismissive "Who knows?", but the more I thought about it, the more I realized I didn't really *want* to return to my old life. Ever.

Don't get me wrong. Spending Thanksgiving with both families and seeing old friends was a delight. We did a little juggling and finagled two fabulous Thanksgiving feasts. Mom's roast turkey was magnificent, and Dick's mother's turkey stuffing—moist, and with just the right amounts of celery and sage—was superb. We enjoyed familiar holiday traditions: traipsing through downtown Minneapolis to enjoy the colorful Christmas lights on Nicollet Avenue and the old-fashioned window displays in Dayton's, Powers, and Donaldson's department stores. We went out on the town one night, enjoying a wonderful meal with a huge circle of friends at The King's Inn in St. Louis Park. As was then the fashion, I wore a crocheted purple mini-skirt, white ruffle-sleeved blouse, and black tights that matched my mod heels. The evening was fun, but after an hour, I began to feel restless.

The experience couldn't compare to the sense of awe I felt while watching the Milky Way spill its luminescence across the northern sky. It felt nothing as satisfying as sipping the morning's first cup of coffee while I sat by a crackling fire planning my chores for the day. I loved my family and friends, but realized, with blinding clarity, that my wilderness experience was changing me. The noise, traffic, and constant go-go-go of city life frayed my nerves. The pressure to dress and act in a certain way made me antsy and irritable.

One frigid Minneapolis morning, as I waited on a downtown corner for Dick to pick me up after a dental appointment, a new self-awareness struck.

I was wearing my fashionable suede boots and an equally stylish white-and-gray checked wool cape that I'd stored in my mother's upstairs bedroom. Now, as I waited for my ride, my legs, covered only by a thin pair of black tights, were freezing. Why hadn't I dressed in my warm wilderness jacket and heavy boots as I would have at the cabin? I knew the answer. I wanted to look stylish. Was that a good reason to freeze my legs off?

Dick turned the corner, and I couldn't jump into the warmth of the car fast enough.

"Am I glad to see you!" I turned up the heater. "My legs feel like popsicles."

"Why didn't you wear your Sorels?" Dick smiled as he shifted gears and we moved down Nicollet. "Why didn't you wear your warm winter jacket?"

I ignored him, took off my boots and massaged my frozen toes. But I thought about his question as we drove down Portland to visit Dick's parents. Why did I conform the minute I returned to city life? Why hadn't I worn sensible clothes in Minneapolis? A flood of homesickness for our cabin washed over me. I couldn't wait to return to the wilderness where I could sort out my feelings in the quiet and solitude of Tucker Lake.

Now, on this winter afternoon, as we approached the last leg of our journey, I looked forward to being back in our tiny but cozy cabin. I placed a SuperValu bag of groceries into the small space left in the sled and told myself it wouldn't be long before we'd be home. Our plan was to make two quick trips via snowmobile through the woods, bringing food and supplies to the cabin. The task should easily be finished before sunset.

Before leaving for the Thanksgiving holiday, we had made the decision not to travel over the lake ice when we returned. It would have been easier than going through the woods, but we wouldn't have any way of knowing if the ice was safe. The sensible thing to do was to use the overland path.

Dick started the snow machine with a roar, and I hopped on the sled and called a cheerful "C'mon, girl" to Nooky who was running alongside. With a whump the snowmobile pulled the sled forward, and we began our overland trek to the cabin. We flew over the snow for twenty feet before coming to the first rise in the ground. Then, everything went wrong.

The snowmobile and sled bogged down and stopped with a thump. Too late, we realized that the small snowmobile, though repowered by Dick with a bigger engine, still didn't have enough oomph. Too late, we understood that we should have brought snowshoes and broken a better trail through newly fallen snow.

I felt like sitting down in the snow and crying.

"I'll give it more gas," Dick called and punched the throttle. The snowmobile tracks churned in the snow, but nothing moved. He tried again. Nothing. We were hopelessly bogged down.

This could mean only one thing, and we both knew it. We'd have to slog through the woods on foot and make repeated trips, carrying as much as possible each time, especially the perishable food—apples, carrots, and eggs. We couldn't leave the produce we'd bought at low city prices to freeze in the car. Tears filled my eyes, but I squeezed them shut. No time to be a baby.

I could see Dick's face set in grim determination. I gritted my teeth. We spent the rest of that December afternoon trudging back and forth through the snow-filled winter forest with fully laden backpacks. It wasn't fun, but we'd done it before.

When we finally sat before the crackling fire, with everything safely tucked into the cabin, I let out another big sigh of relief. Though the afternoon had been difficult, I felt proud. And content. Things I hadn't felt back in the city.

I was in the right place for me.

13

EARLY WINTER

Nooky, our malamute, her tan fur ruffed by the wind, ran alongside the snowmobile as we swooped down the long driveway to Loon Lake Lodge. Several days had passed since our return from Thanksgiving in the city. After all the travail of hiking in our supplies upon our return, Dick tested the lake ice the next day and found it was thick enough to be safe.

"We could have come in over the lakes," he announced, entering the cabin along with a flurry of cold wind, his wool cap covered with frost. "But we always seem to do things the hard way."

I couldn't argue with that and went back to peeling potatoes.

He spent the rest of the day marking an ice trail across Tucker and Little Iron, and the next day we were able to travel via snowmobile from the cabin to the Gunflint Trail in twenty minutes.

We'd been invited for dinner at Loon Lake Lodge, where Dick had promised Willard he'd help him fix his snowmobile. The Johnsons had moved from the huge main lodge into "The Shack"—a large warm cabin with comfortable chairs and sofas—to spend the winter. We'd visited before. The piles of paperbacks, read by Will, that filled end tables and shelves added to the cozy atmosphere. A gigantic stone fireplace stood at one end of the main room; handy pegs near the front door held coats, scarves, and hats; and the log walls spoke nostalgically of a much earlier era.

As our snowmobile pulled up to the cabin's front door that day, Bumper, a large male collie, rounded the corner, tail wagging. He's gotten his name due to his poor eyesight. He carried his ten years with dignity, taking seriously his duties as all-around lodge-dog. He greeted people, politely allowed children to pet him, and during the summer chased off any unfortunate bear that hoped to steal food from the lodge.

Bumper was legendary for his bear-chasing prowess. Lodge guests wakened by fierce, high-pitched barks knew Bumper was hot on the trail of a bear. The amazing thing was that in spite of his impaired sight, he was a whirlwind.

Maybe it was his undaunted bravery that so attracted our little malamute to the big guy; whatever the reason, she was madly in love. Now as he approached us, Nooky rocketed her six-month-old body at him, squealing and squirming with delight, trying to lick his mouth.

Bumper, as always, wanted nothing to do with her. He turned his long, aristocratic muzzle this way and that to avoid her tongue and would gladly have climbed a tree to escape her passionate attentions. Nooky, oblivious to this rebuff, continued her efforts to charm him, hoping that this might be the day she would win his affections. How could anyone resist her charming face with its black mask and mischievous brown eyes? But Bumper did not capitulate, and after greeting us, he tried to sneak off to a hiding place somewhere behind the cabin.

His effort to ditch Nooky failed. Blissfully in love, she followed with wagging tail and stuck to him like glue during the entire visit. We went inside the cabin, enjoyed a meal of scalloped potatoes and ham, and watched a Vikings football game.

When it came time to go, we found Nooky still stalking her adored but standoffish Bumper.

We hopped on the snowmobile, but I had to call Nooky several times before she grudgingly followed us, her ears flattened to her head, as Dick throttled the snowmobile up the driveway. Watching us leave, Bumper perked his ears, and I swear I saw a smile on his face as we took the pesky puppy away.

Several days later, Nooky went into heat. "This can't be!" I shouted. "She's only six months old!" Nooky was in estrus, or as Dick so delicately put it, "had attained womanhood."

This was a nuisance, but tolerable. What concerned me was that the locals at Loon Lake Lodge had filled our heads with frightening stories of wolves mating with dogs. We were told that male wolves are attracted to female canines in heat. The resulting half-wolf-half-dog could be troublesome and downright dangerous. Worse still, male wolves had been known to kill female dogs after mating,

It was too late to neuter Nooky at this stage—in any case, we simply didn't have the money for the surgery—so we promised each other to keep a close eye on her. Added to the dozens of winter chores that now filled our days, was the new edict, "Keep an eye on Nooky." As Dick cut and split wood (the deepening cold was taking its toll on the woodpile), kept the snowmobile and chainsaw running, built a wood box, and paneled two cabin walls, he also watched out for Nooky's well-being. I kept track of her as I washed dishes, swept the floor, and filled and carried an assortment of water containers from a hole in the ice. The newly formed ice had created an extra chore: I had to strain every bucket of water to remove the small, almost microscopic, black swimming creatures that had suddenly appeared in it.

I spent a good deal of time preparing meals. My repertoire had expanded with the onset of colder temperatures. Now food could be stored outside in nature's giant freezer. With fresh meat available, I prepared all sorts of meals ranging from hamburger hot dishes and fried chicken to liver and onions. Through this myriad of chores, I also kept an eye on Nooky.

We thought the wolf situation was under control until one morning when Dick took the snowmobile to explore the west end of the lake. Tucker is approximately three miles long and a quarter mile wide, with the west end of the lake abutting the BWCAW. Isolated and rarely visited, this part of the lake is wilder than the rest. On this sunny, cold, morning, as Dick headed west down the middle of our peaceful, snow-blanketed lake, he spotted footprints that clearly weren't deer or moose. Jumping off his machine, he took a closer look and was dumfounded to see huge wolf paw prints.

More ominously, the tracks headed east, towards our cabin. He jumped on his machine, did a U-turn, and followed the tracks, noticing the wolf's yellow calling cards on small bushes at several places along the shoreline. Finally, the wolf tracks turned and disappeared into the woods, barely an eighth of a mile from our cabin.

He rushed home to tell me. "We've really got to keep an eye on her," he insisted, and although he seemed calm as he rubbed Nooky's ears, I knew he was nervous.

I agreed. "The warnings from Willard about wolves..." I didn't finish.

He nodded.

From that point on we no longer allowed her to nestle in her burrow under the cabin, but made her stay inside. We even brought her beloved pink ladybug squeaker toy in from her den outside. Trying to inject some humor into the situation, I said, "Why don't we call the wolf Alphie?" The name stuck.

Several nights passed, during which we saw no further wolf signs. The crisis seemed to be passing. Then, one night, I opened the door to let Nooky out to perform her nightly duty. Her ears perked, and, without warning, she bolted. Her feet hit the ground, her nose flew into the air, and just as she was about to charge out into the darkness, I grabbed her collar, almost missing it.

She whipped her head towards the lake and pulled, giving a low growl. I held tight and glimpsed a shape from the corner of my eye. Or did I? I went into full alert. Was that a dark form I saw down on the shore? I couldn't be sure. It was there one minute and gone the next. Had I seen a wolf?

Taking no chances, I screamed. "Dick, come out here!" I kept clinging to Nooky's collar. Dick ran to the door, shotgun in hand. "What's going on?"

"I saw something dark down on the lake, but I couldn't tell...it disappeared—" I faltered. "But it was *something!*"

I pointed to the spot where the I'd seen the shadow. Dick walked down to the lake to check out the situation, shining his flashlight in circles.

Several minutes passed before he called, "Nothing." Taking no chances, I still held tight to Nooky's collar as I let her perform her nightly duties. When finished, she jumped up to the deck, plumed tail waving.

Dick climbed the small hill from the lake, looking perplexed. "Whatever it was, it's gone."

We speculated as we brushed our teeth and turned off the gas lamps.

"I hope he doesn't come back, if it was Alphie." I pulled up the sleeping bag and settled my head on the pillow, hoping not to dream of wolves and shadowy forms.

Dick agreed. "We don't need a wolf prowling around here."

Next morning, in the first light of day, Dick inspected the lakeshore, and as I splashed my face with warm water from the kettle on the wood stove, I heard his voice.

"Get down here!" he yelled. Dropping my washcloth, I ran out the door and down the hill.

"Look," Dick's voice quavered. Well hidden by the darkness last night but showing up big and bold in the morning sun were large wolf paw prints not more than fifteen feet from the cabin door.

"And look at that!" Dick pointed to a spray of yellow urine on the nearest bush. Alphie had indeed come courting.

"So it was a wolf that I saw last night." The reality was hard to accept. Not that far away, a huge wolf had skulked. It was sheer luck that I'd grabbed Nooky's collar and saved her from running after it.

"We won't be relaxing our vigil yet," I remarked, my lips tightened in grim determination. From that day on, until she went out of heat, we watched Nooky with religious fervor. I finally understood that, truly, we weren't alone. The forest was filled with animals, and they were watching us.

14

WHEREVER I GO, THERE I AM

Eventually, Nooky came out of heat, the wolf scare died down, and we tried to settle into a peaceful routine. Yet, for some reason, Dick and I both felt uneasy.

November's dreary weather added to the feeling, but what bothered me most was the coming holiday season. We'd promised our families we'd return to Minneapolis in two weeks and that we'd stay for the entire week of Christmas celebrations. I felt good about that. What caused my anxiety was the invitation we'd extended to friends to visit us at Tucker.

They planned to arrive the same day we returned from our holiday trip. Although I loved our friends, I fretted, wondering how I was going to unpack, get the cabin warmed, and prep a meal for company after a long day on the road.

Dick was also on edge. His goals were to have a large supply of firewood cut and the snowmobile in good working condition for our visitors. However, these ambitions were being constantly thwarted by mechanical problems.

My biggest goal was to make the cabin more cheerful. I hated its bleak unpainted decor. I wanted the plywood walls to glisten with a fresh coat of paint, maybe a warm color that

Our "living room" after a few months of living and decorating. A cozy Franklin fireplace replaced the old wash stove. I liked the mustardy yellow paint, although I'm not sure Dick ever did.

would lighten the room. Problem was, we didn't have money for extras like paint.

That changed one day as I poked around under the cabin and discovered a gallon of leftover deck paint. I pulled out the can and danced in glee. Here was the solution to my quandary. The yellowish color was a tad dark, but it looked better than the existing walls. Hauling out paintbrushes and thinner, I wasted no time and started painting the interior with the obsessiveness of a marathon runner.

Although my arms ached and the paint fumes invaded our lungs, I worked relentlessly day after day to finish this task.

Dick hated the color. "Looks like mustard," he complained one day while surveying my work.

"It brightens things up," I snapped and stubbornly slapped on another brushload of paint. The cabin was impossible to ventilate properly in the below-zero temperatures, and the fumes were giving me headaches that made me crankier than normal, but I didn't mention them. I had to finish the job, so I convinced myself that the odor would dissipate in a few days.

I kept doggedly painting, ignoring the fumes while Dick cut extra wood and tinkered with the snowmobile. Either the chainsaw broke down or the snowmobile stalled. As the days passed, his anxiety level soared along with mine.

One night my irascibility and Dick's frustrations boiled over. Without intending to, I yanked the comforter from his grasp. This wouldn't have been too bad, but he was just climbing out of bed to put another log on the fire. "What the—!" he yelled, grabbing the bed's rim to save himself from a crash to the floor. He mumbled something I didn't hear but took to be insulting.

"What was that?" I challenged. He didn't answer, but grabbed a log, threw it on the fire, and dropped back into bed with a heavy thud.

I muttered, "Putz," and we both lost it.

I threw my fuzzy pink slipper sock at him, and he yanked the cover from my grasp. I pulled back. *What a jerk*, I thought, as he returned the slipper sock with a throw that bounced off my forehead. That ended our outburst and an icy quiet filled the cabin. I settled down to sulk; he didn't say another word.

When morning broke, gray and dreary, I schlumped about my morning chores silently, plopping his bacon and over-easy eggs in front of him with a thud. He returned the silent treatment as I sat down and chewed on bacon and toast. Even the coffee was bitter that morning. I'd probably dumped in too many grounds—yet one further expression of my sulking and irritation.

The silence continued, along with a wailing west wind, until Dick, dropping his fork on his empty breakfast plate, finally broke the ice. "We should talk." He lifted a cup of hot coffee to his lips.

Anger knotted my stomach, but I managed a reluctant nod. A few minutes later, while pouring coffee into my green and white mug, I decided to spill my guts.

"What's happened to you?" I demanded. "Ever since Thanksgiving, you've been a real pain in the ass."

I could have predicted Dick's response. "What's wrong with *you*? You're no picnic either."

We ranted through six more cups of coffee. At first I felt insulted by his insinuations. "What's wrong with my wanting to make the cabin nicer?" I insisted.

"Nothing," he answered, then added, "well, to tell the truth, the color is butt ugly, but mostly you've been crabby. Not easy to live with."

That inflammatory statement got me going again. "You think you're a barrel of laughs?"

Our battle of insults continued, but our anger dissipated little by little, until, many harsh words later, we finally began to return to our senses. "Maybe I've been putting too much stress on myself getting ready for Christmas," I admitted.

Dick agreed. "I do worry about not have enough firewood when Jon and Rosemary visit." He frowned. "And there's always problems with the snowmobile."

I nodded. "It's pressure. After all, we're out here in the middle of nowhere. Have to fend for ourselves."

"True." He looked into his coffee dregs. "We shouldn't do that to ourselves."

"So true." I agreed.

We agreed that performing the daily tasks of wilderness life—carrying water, cutting firewood—was enough of a challenge in our isolated and primitive conditions without the unnecessary pressures we'd put on ourselves. The solution to our troubles was obvious. "We have to take things as they come," I said. "So what if the walls don't get painted? Does it make that big a difference in the larger picture?"

Dick added his two cents worth. "So what if the snowmobile doesn't run—we could always use snowshoes."

We were alone in the wilderness. "We have to depend on

each other," I took another sip of coffee. "Without meaning to, we went back to our old city ways."

"That kind of 'go-go-go' doesn't work here," Dick agreed.

We clinked our coffee cups. I gave a toast. "Time to slow down and remember why we came."

A weight fell from my shoulders. Dick's relieved demeanor told me he shared my feeling. We smiled at each other as a peace once again filled our one-room home. Just sitting felt wonderful. But eventually, we both started to stir.

"Better get going." Dick finally set down his coffee cup. Throwing on his winter jacket, he walked to the lake with a newfound buoyancy and cranked up the snowmobile. Waving a cheery good-bye, he roared down the lake to pick up the mail. I figuring he'd be back in half an hour unless he stopped to talk to the Johnsons.

Applying the mustardy gold paint to the brush, I smiled. The whole purpose of spending a year in the woods had been to escape from the rat race, and yet, somehow, we had managed to create our own. I remembered a quotation. *Wherever I go, there I am.* How true, I chuckled. It's hard to change old habits.

I've got to stay calmer, take things as they come, I promised myself, then stopped, paintbrush in mid-air. Was that a snowmobile engine reverberating down the lake? I listened more closely. Uh-oh. It was heading in this direction. This wasn't good. Dick hadn't been gone ten minutes. Too early for him to return.

But there he was. The snowmobile stopped on the lake, in front of the cabin. I ran to the door, fighting for composure. "What's wrong?" I called from the deck. He stayed where he was, momentarily motionless.

Finally with a grim face, Dick jumped from the snowmobile and strode up the hill to the cabin. "Slush!" He announced. His eyes were wide and he had trouble catching his breath. "And lots of it. Lucky I didn't get stuck."

"Good thing we had our pep talk this morning," he added,

forcing a smile. I watched, dumbfounded, as he marched to the cabin's south wall, where we kept our snowshoes. It truly was lucky we'd had our talk this morning, or we'd both be off the rails. As it was, I could see that relaxing and accepting this wilderness life would take a lot of determination.

The important thing is that we're both trying, I told myself, watching Dick slide his booted feet into the snowshoe harnesses.

"Let's see if I can tramp over the surface, breaking the snow cover so the water seeps up and freezes overnight to make a path." Stepping carefully down the hill, he gave a cheerful wave to let me know he was trying to stay calm and pointed his snowshoes east with Nooky following.

I watched as he marched down the beautiful but treacherous snow-covered lake, following our marked trail. Dick was coping graciously, and I was trying.

I took another look at his disappearing figure, then trudged back to the cabin, picked up the paintbrush, and finished covering the last little spot on the wall with mustardy gold.

15

Holiday Celebrations

Our Christmas visit was over; the holidays in Minneapolis had sped by. After a day of driving, we were almost home. The problem was that we were stranded in slush, halfway down ice-covered Little Iron Lake, and I was trying with all my heart and soul to stay calm and relaxed. Not easy.

Standing forlornly beside our mired snowmobile and sled, I looked at the deflated expression on Dick's face. Our attempt to cross the lake on our marked ice path had failed. We were stuck.

Any innocent-looking, snow-covered lake can hide lurking slushy water, and any snowmobile not fast enough or big enough will mire down and get stuck. The slush forms when heavy snow depresses the ice, causing water to seep up and flood the ice's surface. The snow hides the slush while also insulating it, which prevents it from refreezing, and that makes for a treacherous situation.

"Now what?" I asked, trying to sound calm, not irritable. I didn't need to ask. We both knew we'd be forced to put on our snowshoes, lift heavy backpacks to shoulders, and hike the remaining two miles to the cabin. We'd let the slush surrounding the snowmobile freeze overnight, then return in the morning and chop it out. I felt downright depressed and angry at Mother Nature.

All my plans were in disarray. I ground my teeth, admitting that obviously I wasn't able to stay calm. We had just spent ten days in the city, celebrating Christmas, and our friends Jon and Rosemary would be arriving any minute. They were skiing at Lutsen, then driving up the Gunflint to stay at our place. I'd hoped we'd get back to the cabin before they arrived so I could warm up a frozen beef and potato casserole for dinner. Well, that plan was down the drain!

I didn't know what to do. Our friends would soon arrive and here we were, stuck in slush. Two weeks earlier we'd left a hard-packed, slush-free ice trail when we took off for Minneapolis, but obviously conditions had changed. And what about their snowmobile? What if they got stuck too?

The afternoon light was dwindling to a pale blue. Anxiety-ridden and wondering why things never seemed to go right, I reached for my backpack but stopped when a new noise caught my ear. Was that a muffled roar? I listened, straining my ears. Could it possibly be our friends? Dare I dream?

Dick heard it, too, and our hope-filled eyes met, then filled with relief as we recognized the sound. It was them. We recognized the roar of their large snowmobile engine. I peered into the distance. Across Little Iron, moving away from the shoreline, a dark object was hurtling towards us.

Our friends, on their huge, twenty-inch tracked Polaris, had arrived. I'd never been happier to see anyone in my life. Relief swelled inside as I watched their machine, with all its oomph and power, float over the lake surface. When they pulled up in a swirl of snow, I plastered them with the biggest hugs I could muster.

Following my enthusiastic welcome and a lot of discussion as to what to do, they motioned me aboard their machine and we scooted to the cabin, where Jon deposited me and Rosemary before returning to help Dick.

As I quickly built a fire and placed the frozen potato-beef casserole to heat on the stovetop, I wondered if the guys would have any luck pulling our snowmobile from its ice prison. But I needn't have worried. Ten minutes later, the roar of two snow-mobiles echoed down the lake. The big Polaris had pulled our Sno-Pony out of the slush, slick as a whistle.

I pulled out a bottle of Chianti to celebrate the occasion.

☙

The adventures continued. The next day Jon and Dick rode their snow machines on the path behind the cabin, while Rosie and I chatted and read magazines in the toasty warm indoors.

We'd barely started talking when our chatter was suddenly interrupted by the roar of returning snowmobiles. We looked up, perplexed. It was much too soon for the guys to be return-ing, but their excited voices filled the air as they stomped into the cabin.

Dick was dripping wet from the waist down. "What hap-pened?" I asked, flabbergasted. "What's with that strange look ?"

A goofy, slapped-alongside-the-head expression crossed both their faces, and Dick, pulling off his wet snowmobile suit, explained. "You know how deep the snow is back in the woods?"

I nodded.

"It was really hard to break trail but we kept pounding through with the Polaris. Finally, when we got to the river, we thought we'd play it smart and take a rest, so we got off our ma-chines. It was kinda nice, no wind and no clouds, and we were just shooting the bull when the ice around me broke."

"Oh my God! You were on the river?"

Dick nodded and continued. "We didn't know what was hap-pening. I thought the river was frozen just fine, but suddenly the ice was cracking and water surging up, and I was in the river."

Rosemary and I leaned forward, stunned.

"Luckily the water was only waist deep. Jon grabbed my hand and pulled me up and we got the hell out of there and off the river. But then," and here Dick and Jon exchanged that goofy look again, "we noticed that Jon's huge Polaris was still resting about a foot from the spot where I fell in. Jon didn't waste a minute. He tiptoed carefully to his machine and held down the throttle while he walked it slowly off the river."

The men exchanged that goofy look again and now I understood. It was an oh-my-god-what-if look.

Since things had ended well we all had a good laugh, but from that point on and for the rest of the year, Dick and I treated the Tucker River with greater respect.

We accompanied Jon and Rosemary to the Gunflint Trail the next morning, said our good-byes, and watched their vehicle disappear. We turned to each other. Time to get back to life on Tucker. It was December 31, 1969, and we planned to spend a quiet New Year's Eve in our cozy cabin. The idea of sitting in front of a crackling fire, enjoying peace and quiet after two weeks of visiting and entertaining, seemed mighty good.

Henning, our eighty-five-year-old Loon Lake Lodge neighbor, had different ideas. When we snowmobiled down the lodge's long driveway to say hello to everyone, we discovered Henning was alone. Willard was in Duluth and Kermit in Grand Marais. A wiry man, slightly stooped with age, Henning poured us each a cup of coffee. As we sipped, he leaned back in his favorite armchair, and a hopeful look crossed his wrinkled face. "Why don't you come for dinner? See in the new year," he said in his thick Swedish accent. He nodded his head (covered with an amazing thick mane of white hair) toward the kitchen and added, "I'm making a big kettle of soup."

We exchanged glances. What could we do? Anybody with half a heart couldn't leave the poor old guy alone on New Year's Eve. We said yes but told Henning we needed to go home first and get some chores done.

"We'll come back around dark," I promised. "We'll celebrate the new year."

As we rode the snowmobile up Loon Lake's hill, I told Dick, "He won't last much past nine o'clock, and we'll easily be home by ten."

We returned to Henning that late afternoon, bursting through his log cabin doors on the wings of a frigid wind to the delicious aroma of homemade beef vegetable soup. I set a loaf of my homemade bread on the counter, salivating at the thought of dipping a thick slab into the tasty soup. "Shall we eat?" I looked hopefully at Henning. I was starving.

But he had different ideas.

"Here," he held up a bottle of brandy. "We have to celebrate." And he poured us each a generous amount.

Never much of a brandy drinker, I slowly sipped from my glass. Henning noticed and said, "I know some of you ladies don't have much to do with alcohol. That's okay."

I realized he was thinking of the women of a bygone era, but I didn't correct him. This helped me escape the generous dispensing of booze that Henning seemed to feel was his duty. Dick drank enough to keep the old guy company while Henning relished his evening.

Eventually, I sliced the bread, and we helped ourselves to generous bowls of soup, thick and savory with carrots, cabbage, potatoes, and chunks of beef. Time passed quickly as Henning told stories of his life; how he left Sweden to come to America and work on the docks in turn-of-the-century West Duluth.

Nine o'clock came and went, and the evening began to drag. I realized we wouldn't be escaping early or easily. I hid my yawns, wondering how an eighty-five-year-old could be so lively while all I wanted at age twenty-six was my nice warm bed. He expounded his views, his dislike of big government, organized religion, his belief in socialism. He was having a whoop of a time with us as captive audience.

Ten o'clock passed. I poured half my drink down the sink on a trip to the bathroom, but Henning refilled my glass when he saw it was empty. Apparently he'd forgotten that "ladies don't like alcohol." "Never thought I'd live to see 1970," he exulted in a quavering voice that belied his astonishing stamina.

When a furtive glance at my watch told me that the eleventh hour had come and gone, I worried. Should we stay the night, place the sofa cushions on the floor and sleep? "What are we going to do?" I asked Dick while our host was in the bathroom.

"He's determined to see in the new year."

"Maybe we should stay the night. Sleep on the floor," I suggested with no enthusiasm. "It's starting to snow."

We looked at each other. Nah. No overnight. We wanted to get home.

Finally the clock struck midnight. Henning raised his glass in jubilation. "It's good to be alive," he rejoiced. But he raised no objections ten minutes later when we told him we had to go. He was finally ready for bed.

Leaving leftover homemade bread and cookies for Henning to enjoy in the morning, we bundled in warm clothes, and bidding a final "Happy New Year," Nooky and I hopped in the sled, and Dick started the snowmobile.

Bouncing through the frosty air, we crossed the Gunflint Trail, moved quickly across Little Iron on our marked trail, and soon found ourselves traveling down Tucker. The snowflakes falling when we left Loon Lake Lodge now thickened, forming a curtain that filled the air. My elation at going home suddenly faded. This was worrisome. I watched closely for the broken tree branches that marked our trail.

I didn't see any.

Grimly, we moved forward through the veil of white. "Keep an eye out!" Dick called through the dark night. I peered ahead, hoping we were traveling in the right direction. Hard to know with all the blackness and swirling snow filling the dim snowmobile light beams. A small shiver of fear ran down my spine.

Minutes later, Dick stopped the machine. "We just crossed our own tracks." He shouted back to me. I swallowed. That wasn't good.

"What happened?" I called from the sled. His dark form was almost completely hidden by the thickly falling snow.

"Must have gone in a circle." His voice was almost lost in the wind. "Good thing we noticed the tracks or they'd be covered with snow in minutes and we'd have kept going God knows where."

"*Now* what do we do?" The icy fear moved to my stomach and formed a knot. I pulled my heavy wool cap farther down on my forehead, trying to stave off an ice cream headache from the cold.

Were we lost? How could we be lost? It hadn't felt like it. Hard to believe one minute we were heading home with full confidence in our whereabouts and the next, we didn't know where we were.

The snow stung my cheeks as I searched the dark. I assumed we were on our marked trail, but again, peering through the dark night, saw no tree branch markers.

"What do we do?" I repeated, stifling an inner scream.

Dick was quiet, and we silently peered into the dark, snow-filled night, searching for a familiar landmark. Nothing. Nothing but swirling snow. The knot in my stomach grew. This was something that happened to other people, not us.

Suddenly Dick called, "Look!"

For a brief moment the falling snow stopped, and to our right, we caught a glimpse of spruce tree outlines. "Shoreline!" I yelled. It was our first piece of luck.

"Hang on!" Dick putt-putted the snowmobile and sled over to the shore's edge, where he stopped. We looked at each other.

"Now what do we do?" I felt exhausted.

"Keep our eyes peeled." Dick added. "We'll slowly follow the shoreline. It should take us home."

"We just don't know how far," I said.

Tucker is three miles long. If we were on the side opposite from our cabin, we might have to circumnavigate almost the entire lake before reaching home.

"At least the snow is tapering off." Dick pressed the throttle and we moved slowly along the shore. Five minutes later we saw a familiar sight—the rocks that formed a small cliff-like area where the lake narrowed. Second piece of luck.

"We're at the Narrows," Dick shouted, jubilant. That meant half a mile from the cabin. "Now we know exactly where we are. Pay attention, and we'll be home soon."

I breathed a tentative sigh of relief, but, as our snowmobile slowly moved forward, the snow curtain dropped once again, surrounding us with heavy white waves. Getting lost would be so easy, I tried not to think about it.

We crept through the snowy dark at a snail's pace, making sure the shoreline remained visible to our right.

Finally I recognized the dark form of our cabin—a beautiful sight. When we pulled up and saw that we were home, I wanted to cry from happiness. Although we'd traveled only a half mile from the Narrows, it had seemed like a hundred.

The night wasn't over. Greeted by a frigid cabin, we spent the next hour building a fire and warming ourselves. My hands still shook, and I felt wired. "Want a cup of tea to relax?" I asked Dick.

"Nah," he answered, reaching for the bottle of wine, left over from Jon and Rosemary's visit. "Pour a glass for me, too," I said.

16

Short Days, Long Nights

With New Year's Eve behind us, we blasted full speed ahead into January, the coldest month of the year. Temperatures typically ranged from a balmy +10°F to a frigid -40°F. On one occasion the thermometer read -50°F.

Each day began early, not much after midnight, when Dick rose from our warm bed and made the first of three nightly excursions to feed wood to the fire. These nights of interrupted sleep didn't exactly thrill us, but nothing else worked.

We experimented one night and let the fire go out. "Maybe getting up in a cold cabin won't be all that bad," Dick said. After a full night of uninterrupted sleep, we woke to cold gray ashes in the fireplace and a frigid floor. Skim ice had formed on the drinking water. Without a fire in the hearth, the inside of the cabin felt dreary and depressing. "Not such a great idea," he admitted as we struggled to get ice cold clothes on with stiff fingers. Even my boots felt glacial.

From that point on, Dick rose three times each night to stoke the embers with wood chunks and keep the cabin toasty warm. Because he was the one who got up during the nights, I let him sleep in the mornings while I prepared for the day ahead.

On this early January Sunday, I slipped out of bed. The room temperature was still a bit frosty, so I wasted no time getting dressed. After slipping into jeans and a sweatshirt, I pulled on a thermal quilted jacket and matching pants and stepped into cozy Sorel boots. The sun rose about the same time I did, around quarter to eight, and I was happy to see the early rays striking the treetops out the back window. I stirred the fire's glowing red embers and plopped on two more pieces of split wood.

The thermometer outside the window showed a pleasant -1°F. I trekked to the outhouse, still a platform with a stool. The lid's underside was frost-covered, as usual, and a vision of outhouse walls came to mind, not for the first time. But that project, I knew, would have to wait while we attended to more pressing needs.

As I sat in my open air "bathroom" contemplating the day, I realized that I didn't really mind it that much. I was happy the six inches of snow on the pine bough that had fallen on my exposed derriere two days ago no longer posed a threat. It was a brisk morning, yes, but it could have been thirty degrees colder.

When my outhouse oblations were completed, I trekked swiftly back to the cabin with Nooky at my heels. After washing my hands and face in a stovetop basin of warm water, I turned my full attention to fixing coffee and breakfast. Dick dragged his body from under the covers, and with sleep-filled eyes, stood up. Nooky nosed my knees, demanding her morning meal, now, so I filled her bowl with kibbles, and she gulped down her food with black ears perked.

Reaching into the bottom of the pantry (which now served as a refrigerator since its floor temperature stayed cold), I grabbed a slab of bacon, pulled off six strips, and flopped them into the cast-iron frying pan I had set to heat on the Coleman stove. They began to sizzle, and soon their salty aroma filled the room. When the last piece had firmed and turned crispy brown,

I placed the bacon on a tin plate and set it on the fireplace top to keep warm.

Next, I broke two eggs into the bacon fat and fried them until the yellow yolks glazed, then flipped them with a spatula in the "over easy" fashion. While they finished frying, I toasted homemade bread on a pyramidal camping toaster, worth its weight in gold. The bread had to be turned frequently to become a uniform golden brown, but I preformed this task every morning and could do it in my sleep.

Once Dick had returned from the "outhouse," he washed his hands and face and sat down to breakfast. We ate with gusto, and between bites we discussed the coming day.

Dick started to say something, but I held up my palm. "Wait a minute," I said, then poured us each a cup of steaming hot coffee.

He started again. "I'm going to make sure the snowmobile is working so nothing goes wrong when we go to Loon Lake this afternoon. What time are we supposed to be there ?" We'd been invited there to watch the Vikings play the Kansas City Chiefs.

"Three." I answered, sipping my coffee. "I'm bringing the brownies I baked yesterday. They invited us to dinner again, so I think we should bring something."

We chatted, finished our food, and gulped another cup of coffee. I loved the snug coziness of our little home, especially on frosty mornings. Eventually Dick sighed and reached for his coveralls. "Better start. I need to cut more firewood, too."

"Chainsaw still working?" It frequently broke down, which wasn't surprising given the amount of work it was called upon to do.

"Still working." He held up two crossed fingers, then added. "Oh, and if I disappear down the lake, I'm just checking our ice trail for slush."

Standing up, I said, "I won't worry unless you're gone too long." We went our separate ways, while Nooky slipped out the door with Dick and crawled into her cozy nest under the cabin.

I poured warm water into my dishpan and scoured the plates of bacon fat and egg yolk. The warm soapy water felt good. When I'd put away the breakfast dishes, I carried five empty gallon containers—a motley assortment of old orange juice bottles and camping containers—out to a hole cut in the ice and filled them, using a large ladle to scoop up the water. The ice hole narrowed daily, and eventually this task took more than an hour, and which point Dick would reopen the hole with his ice auger.

Fortunately Dick had recently re-widened the hole; today's water gathering went smoothly. As I scooped water from the hole I enjoyed peering down into the dark water, wondering if any fish lurked there. When my containers were full, I carried them one by one up to the cabin, trying not to slosh the precious water onto the snow.

After the last jug was safely inside, I breathed a sigh of relief—water gathering was my least favorite chore—and hauled out my broom to give the cabin floor a sweeping. Bits of sawdust, pine needles, and Nooky's fur always found their way in, so it needed a daily cleaning.

With that chore finished, I wiped down the ashes that had accumulated on the Franklin stove's surface and cleaned the hearth until the black stove shone in the sunlight.

Checking the slop pail under the counter, I found it didn't need emptying, but the garbage was starting to smell, so I placed another piece of wood on the fire, waited till it glowed red, then threw the small bag on it, quickly closing the doors to let it burn. We tried not to accumulate too much debris, reusing grocery bags and cans and throwing scraps out for the birds, but sometimes the only way to dispose of garbage was to burn it.

The cabin was a toasty temperature by noon when Dick returned, announcing, "I'm starved. What's for lunch?"

Since I spent many hours baking—bread, cookies, cakes,

Winter transport

brownies, you name it—I was ready for him. I reached for the loaf of homemade sourdough bread, cut thick slices, and slathered them with peanut butter. When we'd chomped down several sandwiches apiece, I brought out some homemade donuts for dessert. It amazed me that we didn't gain weight, but the calories seemed to fly off as we went about our daily life.

Dick bundled up again and went out to fine-tune the snowmobile and load up the sled with emergency equipment: a flashlight, a picaroon, and an ax. I cleaned up lunch dishes, packed the brownies, and filled our emergency ditty bag with a set of extra clothes (in case we somehow got wet), candles, and matches.

We planned to leave for Loon Lake around 2:30 and not return until well after dark. We had also decided to leave the party early if snow started falling, not wanting to repeat our recent "lost" episode.

When we finally headed down Tucker Lake, we were well prepared, a good thing in this frozen wilderness where the sun began its slide into the west early and darkness fell by four o'clock.

Today's visit to Loon Lake Lodge was typical. We walked into The Shack, hung our winter garb on the pegs near the front door, and stepped into the main living quarters, where a fire was cracking in the large stone fireplace, its yellow flames reflecting off the log walls.

We drank Chianti, feasted on Will's famous lasagna (a yummy recipe with Velveeta, American, and mozzarella cheeses that I still use), and watched the Vikings lose to the Chiefs. Our neighbor Al appeared out of the dark night to join the festivities, his little Chihuahua tucked into his jacket. After watching the game, we tuned in *The Ed Sullivan Show* to see Tiny Tim and his new bride, Vicki.

The party ended around eight o'clock. Dick went out to rev up the snowmobile, I stood in the sled, and Nooky ran alongside as we disappeared into the dark night.

17

FROZEN RIDE AND NEW STOVE

January continued, frigid and harsh. On this particular morning, the cold was more intense than usual. By noon, I'd finished all my chores, so when Dick popped his head in the doorway and asked, "Wanna go out to the mailbox?" I was ready for action.

The only thing was, the therm ometer read -25°F. Add the wind and a moving snowmobile, and the wind chill would be downright dangerous. At -25°F, water thrown from a glass will freeze before it hits the ground. Although worried about the danger of venturing out in the severe cold, I gave the idea a few minutes of careful thought and decided to go. I'd wear ultra-warm clothes and use common sense.

Mail was delivered three times a week on the Gunflint Trail, and much as I loved our life in the woods, I cherished hearing from home. Only Dick's father and my brother had written recently, so I was hoping today's mail would bring a glut of new letters.

I expended a lot of energy getting into my "winter traveling ensemble." First I pulled on wool long underwear, itchy but warm. I added jeans, a turtleneck, and thermo/quilted outerwear. All this went under a knee-length winter jacket.

Two layers of wool socks in my Sorels, a black woolen face mask, and a heavy wool stocking cap followed. A 3M nose/mouth mask and goggles were my next armaments against the cold. Finally, I covered my hands with leather "choppers" fitted over heavy wool mittens. Once donned, my cold weather outfit was so warm I'd break into a sweat if I dilly-dallied inside.

Looking and feeling like the Pillsbury Doughboy, I executed a clumsy leap into the sled, Dick started the snowmobile engine, Nooky ran in circles barking, and we took off with a roar.

For five delusional minutes, I fooled myself into thinking this wasn't too bad. The sky was blue. The sun shone. I congratulated myself on knowing how to dress for the cold.

We flew down the lake following our ice path. No slush today since no recent snow had fallen and the subzero temps kept everything frozen. But I could tell almost immediately that I was beginning to lose heat. By the time we reached the portage, my fingertips were numb. That was no problem. I knew what to do and curled my hands into fists to keep them warm.

Now my toes hurt. I wiggled them inside the thick felt liners of my Sorels, and they felt better.

Nooky, sturdy dog of the north, ran steadily, tail wagging with happiness. She was built for this weather. Her coat was thick, even her toes were fur-lined. She was in her element.

When we reached the mailbox, I was disappointed. No letters, although the *Minneapolis Tribune* Sunday edition had finally arrived.

"Let's say hello to Loon Lake Lodge," Dick yelled. "And warm up," he added.

Off we whooshed down the long, curving driveway. When we arrived at The Shack, Willard hauled out coffee mugs, and we joined him, Kermit, and Henning in their warm kitchen.

The conversation rambled from snow depth, below-zero

temperatures, and recipes to bottled gas and stoves. I mentioned that I fixed all our meals on a Coleman camp stove that operated by pumping pressure into the fuel tank before it could be lit. "Gotta admit, pumping that Coleman's really built up my right arm muscles," I said.

Kermit's face lit up as he remembered something, and then he offered me one of the best gifts I received all year. He'd put some old but workable stoves in storage when the lodge remodeled their cabins. "Would you like a four-burner propane stove top?" he asked. "It needs cleaning but should work just fine."

"Would I like one? I'd love one," I gushed, and that was settled. We finished our coffee, bundled into our warm clothes again, and followed him to an old garage. From the shadows in the rear of the building he hauled out a slightly rusted four-burner propane grill. It was beautiful.

A year before, I'd have turned up my nose at the old, grit-covered cooktop standing before me, but after far too many pumping sessions on the Coleman, it looked wonderful. We tied it down in the sled, waved a cheery good-bye, and with an extra thank you, started home.

The day had grown even colder. We crossed the portage, snow chunks crackling under the snowmobile runners. As we headed down the three-mile homestretch of Tucker Lake, I knew that if we had engine trouble or got stuck in snow, we'd be in a dangerous situation.

Even Nooky's usual happy "doggie" smile turned grim as she churned through the snow, but she kept pace with the sled as we chugged through a barren white landscape under an icy, pale blue sky. I kept track of her, making sure she stayed with us, although my frost-covered eyelashes cut down my vision.

When we finally pulled up to the cabin, my cheeks were ice-cube cold in spite of the face mask. I couldn't feel my fingers, and my toes were numb. Hunching my entire body against the frigid cold, I jumped off the sled and made a beeline for the cabin.

Nooky rolled and buried her muzzle in the snow, rolled some more, and disappeared into her favorite spot under the cabin, where she curled up and covered her nose with her tail. Eventually we called her inside, and she appeared with her beloved pink ladybug in her mouth.

The fire had gone out, and the inside temperature read 25°F. "Can you believe it?" I said to Dick, who was stomping his boots to get feeling back in his feet. "It's so cold outside that 25 degrees feels warm."

Without wasting a minute, Dick carried my new stove from the sled while I tended the fire, and soon a warm glow filled the room. Only then did I look at my "used" stove. Dick had muscled it through the door and set it on the floor to better scrutinize. I couldn't have been happier if someone had given me the latest stove model in *Better Homes and Gardens*. Every inch was covered in grime, especially the burners, but they were a convenient size and the knobs turned easily. It looked wonderful.

As twilight deepened from blue to black, Dick split wood, filled the wood box for the night, and made sure the kerosene lamps were full. Resigned to a few more days of the old routine, I huffed and puffed while pumping up the Coleman, lit it, and fried hamburgers for supper, dreaming of the not-too-distant day I could use my new stove.

18

FUDGING AROUND

During the darkest January days, dusk crept in early and evenings were long, but we were never bored. We listened to our favorite radio station, WGN Chicago. Tonight we followed a Black Hawks hockey game.

Nestled in my chair near the warm fireplace, I wrote my weekly letter to my folks describing my "new" old stove. Dad would get a kick out of my humble lifestyle since throughout my teen years, I'd dramatically vowed that someday I'd marry a rich man and live in New York City. *But here I am*, I thought, as I sealed the envelope, *poor as a church mouse and happy. Who would have thought?* Picking up one of the many books I'd checked out from the Grand Marais Library, I pulled up my chair, moved my feet nearer to the fire, and began reading.

Dick had installed small gas lamps that made the cabin's interior much brighter. Before that, kerosene lamps had been our only light source. I loved their coziness but had to admit that the new modern lamps made reading and writing much easier.

This evening, he leaned back in his chair on the other side of the fireplace carving a woodland scene out of a chunk of wood.

Half an hour passed quietly, interrupted only by the sounds of a knife crossing wood and the occasional rasp of a turning page. Dick's face knotted in concentration as he made cuts here and there, carefully sculpting until the shape of a pine tree emerged.

Without warning, he jumped up, set down his carving and said, "Let's make fudge."

"Good. I'll get the ingredients." I slammed my book shut and leaped from my chair.

Dick had grown up in a fudge-making family and had introduced me to this tradition. When we lived in the city, he'd tried to tutor me in the art of fudge making, but I'd always been happy to let him take over. At Tucker, without ringing telephones or alluring television programs for entertainment, I came to enjoy the entire process.

I gathered the ingredients and hauled out the aluminum pot, proud of my growing candy-making skills. As we melted the sugar, water, syrup, and chocolate, then let the bubbling mass simmer until it reached soft-ball stage, I was almost convinced that my talents were now equal to Dick's. I'd purchased a candy thermometer in Grand Marais, but Dick used the old-fashioned method his mother had taught him—dropping a fudge glob into cold water. If it turned into a soft but malleable ball, the fudge had cooked to the correct temperature. It sounds simple but recognizing just the right consistency isn't easy.

Once the syrup had simmered for a while, Dick pulled out a dollop with a spoon and dropped it into a water-filled coffee cup.

"Test it," he said.

"You do it," I protested, "You're the expert."

"No, really. You know how," he insisted and pushed the cup closer. What the heck. I rolled the test fudge between my fingers. It formed a sloppy round shape. Was this enough? Should it be firmer? Softer? Dick watched. I agonized. Was this the elusive "soft ball" stage? I had to made a decision.

"Yes. It's good." I declared. Dick tossed another small blob of fudge into the water, testing it for himself.

"Good to go!"

I ran into the frigid night with an empty dishpan, filled it with snow, then brought it in. Dick set the hot syrupy pot of unfinished fudge in the snow-filled pan, and we waited for it to cool.

This step took the most patience. The sugar-syrup-chocolate mixture had to cool gradually before we added the butter and vanilla and stirred the whole concoction. This part always seemed to take forever. I went back to my book and waited for the stuff to cool. But I couldn't stand the waiting and soon I was poking the end of a wooden spoon into the sugary chocolate mass. Still too hot. Returning to my book, I waited five long minutes before testing again. Still too hot. Dick reassessed his wood carving and took off a few more paper-thin layers of wood.

We checked two more times until finally, after almost an hour, Dick touched the chocolate mass and yelled. "It's cool! Get to work!" The final stage—beating the fudge with a wooden spoon—needed to start immediately. We took turns mixing the shiny brown mass. Dick did most of the work, but during my turns with the mixing spoon I held out as long as I could to give him a break before he had to take over again.

Finally, the chocolate mass turned dull, a sign that it was hardening.

"It's ready!" I whooped.

"Quick!" Dick yelled. The chocolaty syrup became harder by the second as we struggled to pour it from the cooking pot into a greased pan. I held the pot, gripping as hard as my fingers allowed, while Dick scooped the hardening chocolate mass into a greased pan as fast as he could.

Finally we scraped the last bit of fudge from the pot and smoothed it down. We had done it, but one question remained.

"Think it'll be creamy?" I asked.

"Never know till you try it." Dick took out a knife, cut two squares, and handed one to me.

This was the true test. Would the fudge be creamy, with a melt in-your-mouth consistency, or had we cooked it too long, in which case it would be dry and crumbly?

We put the squares into our mouths simultaneously, looking deep into each other's eyes. The fudge melted on my tongue. Velvety and intensely chocolatey.

"Fantastic," I crooned.

"Good." Dick agreed. The fudge was perfect.

&

A belly full of fudge didn't make for good sleeping. "Let's take a snowshoe walk," Dick suggested, as we washed and dried the dirty fudge-making pans.

"Perfect," I agreed. We stepped outside into the moonlight, donned our snowshoes, and tromped through the snow down to the shore of the lake. The air was cold and clear, and the newly fallen snow glistened while stars glittered in the black winter sky overhead. The night was breathtaking.

We'd barely covered a fourth of a mile when I heard a noise. I stopped. Dick and Nooky halted too. We listened. The noise echoed down the frozen lake again; a high, somewhat wailing sound. Was it a wolf? The noise wasn't a howl, but...

It was coming from the east. Then we heard it coming from the west. A wolf couldn't possibly have covered that much distance in a few short minutes, but a winged creature could. Or maybe there were two?

"Owl," I said, and Dick agreed. "It's an owl."

We snowshoed well down the lake that night accompanied by those ethereal hoots.

19

A New Era

"We're half-way through our adventure," I wrote in my journal under the heading *February*. "In six months we'll be out of money and forced to return to civilization and take jobs." A sobering thought.

With a sigh, I accepted reality. Time to start sending Dick's job résumé around. He had earned his teaching degree in Industrial Arts and was also a certified scientific glassblower. We were hoping that with a combination of a college degree and a trade, he'd have no trouble finding a job, ideally one that would start in late summer.

It had become clear in the course of our experiment that the woods suited us better than a metropolis like Minneapolis. A small city that offered both a quiet lifestyle and the benefit of good jobs might be a good choice for a permanent home: Duluth, Rochester, Sioux Falls, maybe Madison. During our morning coffee times, we'd discussed various alternatives and agreed we'd return to Minneapolis only if nothing else worked out.

Yes, I needed to start polishing résumés, but not today. I pushed the bothersome thought from my mind. Finishing my journal entry, I glanced around the cabin, wondering if I should bake more bread to go along with the meatloaf I was fixing for dinner. Suddenly the cabin door flew open, bringing a burst of cold air along with Dick.

"Got enough wood split?" I asked.

"Yeah. But I was thinking it'd be a perfect day to ski down to Loon Lake Lodge when I get the mail. Want to go?"

The lodge had a steep, winding, switchback driveway that the Johnsons closed for the winter when they parked their vehicles on the Gunflint Trail. Their shut-down driveway made a good ski run. Several times this past month we'd stepped into our downhill skis and sped down the hill with satisfying whooshes.

"Why not? It's gorgeous out." This was one of the things I loved about our life in the woods. We could do whatever we wanted on the spur of the moment. I grabbed my outdoor garb from the hook near the door.

Half an hour later, we were zooming down the white surface of Tucker Lake, skis bungeed to the sled and Nooky bounding alongside, white plumed tail wagging in ecstasy.

We reached the Gunflint Trail and Dick retrieved our mail. I watched as a car picked up speed and disappeared around the bend. "Wonder who that was?" I said.

"Looks like they might have been here." Dick shielded his eyes from the bright winter sun and handed me a letter, then stuffed the rest of the mail in the backpack. Nooky sniffed the mailbox posts, then disappeared down the driveway, running to find Bumper down at The Shack.

We parked the vehicle in the plowed area in front of an old storage building and got into our skis. Thrusting my hand through the ski pole straps, I followed Dick as he pushed along the flat upper section of the driveway, picking up speed. The winter day was exquisite: blue skies, crisp air, and thick snow on the driveway that made for an exciting run.

Dick, who weighed more than I did, gained speed. I tried to catch up, and turning the first curve I gave an extra hard push.

I was moving into the second turn when I was forced to make a quick stop. Just ahead, Dick had stopped and was talking to someone.

Willard, in the red-and-black flannel shirt he always wore, stood alongside the driveway. "Did you see the car leaving?" Willard asked.

We nodded.

"Had to tell the Whitlaws they couldn't stay at their cabin," he continued, pointing to a log cabin barely discernible through the woods.

I remembered them, a couple in their late fifties or early sixties. Normally they visited their cabin in the summer months.

Willard went on. "Their furnace is fritzed. Funny. I checked it last week when they called to say they'd be up. Worked fine then, but when I tried to get it going this morning, it wouldn't start."

"What a shame," he continued. "They drove all the way from Chicago. They've got friends in Grand Marais they can stay with, but it's still too bad." He shrugged. "You never know about life in the woods."

He picked up his backpack—I could hear tools clanking inside—and started off down the hill. "Come on down for coffee." He gestured towards The Shack.

The Whitlaws and their disappointment stayed on my mind as I skied down, and they stayed on my mind for the rest of the afternoon. I felt so lucky to be having this adventure when I was young.

That evening, getting philosophical as we ate meatloaf, I voiced my thoughts. "I don't want to spend my whole life working in the rat race, grabbing little bits of freedom instead of enjoying a whole feast like we are now."

Dick was more practical. "You know, sooner or later, you and I have to get jobs and join that rat race. We can't live in the woods forever."

"No. We can't do that." I agreed. "That's too risky. One of us has got to get a job, and considering the kinds of work that are available, I think it's going to be you. I'll apply at the school district in Grand Marais, and I'll start typing and sending résumés for you. We'll see what happens."

Dick agreed, and the next morning we began sending out his résumé. I even sent one to McGraw Hill Publishers, who had listed a job selling industrial arts books. It would require relocating to St. Louis, but we reasoned that it would be an entirely new adventure, and therefore worth pursuing.

꙰

The bone-chilling January cold softened as February passed, but February weather could be wildly unpredictable. You had to be ready for anything.

I was thinking about our reliance on nature one afternoon in early February as I grated the last bit of Parmesan cheese onto the lasagna I was prepping for company. The day was glorious. The thermometer read a balmy 40° F. Wispy white clouds floated across a bright blue sky, and the snow sparkled like diamonds.

Neighbors from a nearby resort were coming over for dinner, and we prepared for them in a flurry of activity. Dick swept and cleaned up the cabin while I put together a lasagna dinner and made a quick batch of fudge. As I set the Dutch oven filled with lasagna on the grill over the fireplace coals, I noticed that snowflakes had started tumbling past the window—a sight that I loved. It always made me feel cozy.

But as the aroma of baking lasagna filled the cabin, the snow began falling faster and heavier. By three in the afternoon, Dick pointed to the heavy white blanket that completely obliterated the opposite lakeshore. He walked to the back window and glanced at the outside thermometer. "Temp's dropping too."

An hour later, when bubbling cheese and a toasty brown crust indicated the lasagna was ready, I pulled it out of the fire.

It was done to perfection, but I knew we'd be eating our dinner alone. The wind howled and copious snow piles filled the path to the lake. No one would venture out in this weather.

We ate a quiet meal with the firelight flickering, snow falling, and wind howling, bracing ourselves for a long blizzard siege. But around nine o'clock, the snow and winds subsided. By ten o'clock the storm had moved on and stars began to appear faintly in the dark night sky. By eleven the temperature had plummeted to -30°F, a drop of 70 degrees since noon.

February was a month of sharp contrasts, beautiful sunny days followed by heavy snow, then frigid weather. When the weather was good, it was glorious. When it was bad, it was just plain rotten.

20

PART-TIME WORK

It happened to be a sunny morning with a slight breeze, but we weren't enjoying its beauty. Standing inside a cabin (not ours), staring up at its tall rafters, we were poised at the threshold of a new challenge, and I wasn't thrilled.

The cabin in which we stood, an A-frame construction, was the only other building on Tucker Lake besides ours. It was located a fourth of a mile west of our place, it needed to be torn down, and we had promised we'd do it.

Dick's high school friend and his wife had built the cabin in the early 1960s. Not long after they finished it, the United States Forest Service informed them that it stood on federal land and gave them thirty days to tear it down and clear the property so not a whiff of human contamination remained. If they failed to do so, they would be fined.

However, they were backpacking in Europe at the time, so they contacted Minnesota Congressman Hubert Humphrey who, thankfully, was able to get them a time extension.

When they wrote and asked if we'd be willing to tear down the place, it seemed like a good idea. We'd do it in the winter when a frozen lake would make it easy to transport the salvageable lumber—our reward for undertaking the task—and we could use the wood to add another room to our cabin.

All winter we'd been settling in, focusing on other tasks, and basically procrastinating, but time was slipping by. We'd decided today was the day. I dreaded it but knew we had to get going.

Now we stood, heads tipped back, as we examined a sleeping loft that was almost hidden by shadows in the back quarter of the roof. From there we bought our gaze down to the cabin's stark and deep-shadowed interior. Next our eyes moved down as we our focused on the floor space. Feeling completely overwhelmed, I said. "How are we ever going to do this?"

"One board at a time, dear. One board at a time." Dick didn't seem to be as overcome as I. He merely handed me a crowbar and waved another one over his head. "Let's get going!"

The gloom inside the A-frame matched my inner gloom, and I couldn't hide it. "Think of the bright side," Dick pointed to the pine board rafters and walls. "When we're done, we'll have some nice lumber for the new kitchen I'm building for you."

I perked up. "True," I agreed, still wishing we'd never gotten ourselves in this position. "What'll I do? Carry stuff outside?"

Although the one huge room was sparsely outfitted and our friends had taken some of their belongings, many things remained. Dick glanced around the cavernous space and took a deep breath. "Might as well start somewhere. Get all the household stuff out of here and in one place. Cover with a tarp, maybe under a tree or something."

The idea of spending my day somewhat in the fresh air instead of trapped in a dreary room mollified me somewhat.

While Dick pulled nails from the loft boards, I pulled on work gloves, moved into the rustic "kitchen" area—really just some boards nailed into a makeshift table and counter—and for the next hour I trotted in and out, gathering flatwear, camp plates, and coffee cups together and setting them in a forlorn pile on a tarp under a large spruce tree.

As the morning sun climbed higher, my thoughts turned more insistently toward the homemade bread topped with peanut butter that we'd brought along for lunch, but Dick didn't look eager to stop working, and I decided I'd rather finish this task than eat lunch anyway.

An hour later, I was just setting the final item from the kitchen—a large white metal chamber pot—on the tarp when Dick called from inside. "I need help carrying these boards down to the lake."

"Wow," I said as I looked carefully for the first time at the loft flooring he'd already dismantled and arranged in a pile. "You're speedy." For the next hour, using our snowmobile and sled, we transported the boards down the lake to our cabin.

Now Dick got serious. Crowbar in hand, he pulled out a window, nails squeaking. I brought it down to the sled. Wielding his crowbar again, he removed the front door, and we carried *that* to the sled. Then he looked at me with a satisfied smile and said, "Now on to the roof."

"What?" I said, sweaty and tired. "That's way too much for one day. Come on, let's go home. It's nearly four o'clock."

"Not yet. I want that roof down!" He motioned me aside. "You can't help. Just get out of the way."

I stood near the tarp-covered pile of household utensils and watched as he tugged and pulled, trying to loosen at least one of the pivotal boards. Finally, it budged. "This should get things caving in." He announced confidently.

He gave a good whack at the long boards making up the A shape of the roof, but nothing budged. Hauling out his chainsaw, he started it with a roar and smoothly cut through a load-bearing wall. "Hope this does it!" he yelled, standing back, but the A-frame roof stayed intact.

"That damn thing's never coming down!" I muttered aloud. Ignoring me, he continued pounding and cutting. I moved from the spruce tree to the lake, where I perched on the snowmobile seat and waited. For the next twenty minutes, Dick pounded and pulled, pulled and pounded. The setting sun dropped behind the trees, creating deep blue shadows. With Nooky at my side, I watched. "Never gives up, does he," I muttered to myself wryly.

"I heard that," Dick yelled. "I refuse to wait until tomorrow!" He yelled even louder and gave the wall another good thunk. It was the straw that broke the camel's back.

With a groaning, splintering sound the peaked roof drifted slowly to one side, gained momentum, and finally, with a long, lumbering crash, slowly caved in. Dust flew, boards splintered, red squirrels far back in the forest chirped in alarm. Nooky high-tailed it out onto the lake. When the air finally cleared, the roof was down on the floor. It was a happy sight. I was starving and the light was rapidly fading. I ran up the hill to the wreckage and stared at the tangled mess of boards and nails.

"We did it!" I shouted and danced with glee. Nooky returned from the middle of the lake. "And just in time."

Standing near the cave-in admiring his handiwork, Dick replied, "It's getting dark. And what's this *we* business? I didn't see you in there with a crowbar."

"I was your cheerleader."

"Now you have no excuse," Dick said, gathering his tools and trotting down to the snowmobile. "Rest up tonight. Tomorrow you start pulling nails and moving the rest of the lumber."

Proud of our feat, we snowmobiled back to the cabin. "Too bad we don't have champagne," I said, hauling out a loaf of sourdough for a peanut butter sandwich. But coffee tasted just fine.

For the next three weeks I wholeheartedly jumped into the project, pulling nails and carrying lumber, happy to be outside in the beautiful late winter weather with its bright sunny skies and sparkling white snow. After all, the sooner we got all of this building material back to our cabin, the sooner my dream of an expanded kitchen would become a reality.

21

First Spring

Winter was losing its grip. I no longer needed to light the kerosene lamps at 4:30 in the afternoon. The sky remained bright and the sun didn't set for almost another hour. The beautiful arctic red sunsets of January had been replaced by an evening horizon that glowed in soft apricot shades.

One afternoon, while I was helping Dick carry firewood through the birch trees, the long lovely call of a chickadee caught my ear—not the crisp winter *chickadee dee-dee-dee* song but the sweet fluting birdsong of summer. The notes sent a rush of happiness through me.

I began to notice other things: the sun was now hotter, melting snow that froze at night, turning the lake into a long, smooth walkway. One afternoon we strolled along that walkway, warm breezes touched our cheeks, and sun rays gilded the spruce tops. We passed the steep, rocky bank where turtles sunbathed in summer. We walked past magnificent red pines, a stand of jack pine, all the way down to the scraggly alder brush at the lake's westerly tip.

With the coming of what I called "first spring," we felt a new surge of energy and were filled with ambition. We spent hours discussing building plans for the new ten-by-eight-foot room as enthusiastically as if we'd been planning the design for a Tudor mansion on Lake of the Isles. Dick bustled about, digging holes for the pilings on which the cabin's addition would stand. It would double the size of our living quarters, and that was exciting.

An occasional -20° F morning reminded us that spring hadn't *really* arrived, but deep in our hearts we knew that the worst of winter was over. The sporadic blustery snowfalls didn't dampen our spirits either, because we knew the following day would likely be warmer.

In this "first spring," more people visited. One February day we entertained twelve people. Two acquaintances that Dick used to work with unexpectedly stopped in one morning. We welcomed them with coffee. I knew Gunflint Trail protocol by now. Coffee—always, always offer coffee.

One evening, a group of snowmobilers surprised us with a visit. Somehow, I managed to find enough coffee cups in my small cupboard to serve everyone. The snowmobilers came in the dark, and although I loved wilderness peace and quiet, the roar of engines and the sight of bright headlights approaching out of the black night was dramatic. The group included adults and children, and the enthusiasm with which they described several recent moose sightings was contagious.

When the red taillight of the last machine disappeared into the darkness, Dick and I sat on the deck as a three-quarter moon rose, surrounded by brilliant yellow stars floating in the black sky. These stars were softer and warmer than the high, cold stars of January.

It was a good time to be alive. "First spring" was here. Now we could enjoy the rest of the winter until "second spring"—the real spring—arrived.

Although tearing down the A-frame and our many daily chores kept us busy, we always found time to relax. Dick cut several holes in the ice and rigged up a fishing rod for me, and I began what I imagined would become serious fishing sessions. I brought a camp stool out on the ice, baited a hook, and plopped it down the hole into the darkness below. Then I waited. The sky was a soft blue, the snow-covered shores were pristine, and I realized, sprawling out my legs and tilting my head back, that the white of the lake's snow-covered surface reflected the sun's warmth.

I imagined I was sunbathing on a sand beach. My jacket and snow pants marred that fantasy, but I flung off my jacket and took in the rays that way.

I didn't catch any fish that day, but I caught a great tan thanks to the reflection of snow and ice on a northern lake on a February day. Slowly over the next few weeks, my face and hands took on a golden hue as I fished, and friends began to wonder if I'd vacationed in the tropics. But the tan didn't entirely compensate for the paucity of fish.

❦

I've received some unusual presents during my life, but the Valentine's Day gift Dick gave me that year was one I'll never forget.

My simple present to Dick was an extra-large batch of divinity. He loved the stuff, and I found the task of pouring hot sugar syrup into fluffy beaten egg whites easy enough. I added chopped walnuts to the white concoction, cut and placed the white squares in a heart shape on a plate, and he was happy.

His present for me was a little more complicated. We sat in front of the fireplace each night, reading and listening to the radio, but I yearned for a footstool so I could stretch out my legs and prop up my feet.

For several days, he'd been searching for just the right size log for such a footstool, and on Valentine's Day he found it.

"I'll peel the bark off," he pointed to a nice-looking log, "and cut it to size. Should be ready tonight."

"Make one for yourself, too," I said, feeling generous, and

trekked down to the lake for an extra pail of water to wash the sticky divinity from the cooking pot.

That night, we ate a Valentine dinner of scalloped potatoes and canned ham before exchanging gifts. I handed Dick his plate of divinity, and he presented me with the footstool.

I'd seen him working on it but was amazed at how attractive the finished product looked. Cut to the right height, its peeled sides glistened white and its width looked comfortable. "It's beautiful!" I plunked my feet on it for a try-out. Perfect.

With the dishes washed and put away, I settled in for an evening of serious lounging. With my feet resting on my new footstool, I opened a book and had just finished the first chapter when I glanced down. Something crawled across the top of my footstool, moving very close to my ankles. Something black and shiny with lots of legs.

"Euughhhh!" I screamed, jumping up from my chair.

Another black creature appeared on the log's surface…and another…

"Carpenter ants!" Dick yelled.

"Ugh!" I stared in horror as the cabin's warmth awoke a squadron of ants from their winter hibernation in my lovely footstool. The little black creatures freed themselves from my footstool's interior and, dropping to the floor, circled, looking for a new home.

I was horrified. The ants were bulbously big and shiny black.

"Stand back!" Without hesitating, Dick grabbed my footstool. "Open the door!" He yelled. As the cold air rushed in, he gave a mighty heave and threw my gift into the night.

I have never received a more dramatic Valentine's gift. But when Dick asked me for an idea to replace the footstool, I suggested, "A box of chocolates?"

22

ACCEPTANCES

"Do we really want walls around the outhouse?" Dick asked as he took another sip of coffee.

I looked at him as if he'd grown a third head. Of *course*, I wanted walls around the outhouse. But as I pondered his question, I realized I'd lived through the worst of winter weather without an enclosed outhouse. Did it matter now?

Dick continued: "No walls, no stink—."

Not quite ready to capitulate, I threw out a weak argument. "And no privacy." But I said it without conviction, realizing that quite honestly, I didn't have a strong opinion on the matter.

"Who sees us? Nobody else lives on the lake. If someone's coming by boat, we spot them before they see us. Al is the only one who walks in through the woods, and he rarely visits anymore."

I thought about that. "Well..."

"Besides," Dick offered the deal-maker, "if we left it open for now, it would give me more time to build the new addition."

It was true. I would rather have him complete my new kitchen addition than anything, and I had gotten used to an open-air outhouse. But not all our guests were quite as blasé.

Later in the month, when a former neighbor of Dick's came for a visit, his face registered complete shock when I tutored him on our "outhouse experience."

Handing him a roll of toilet paper, I pointed to the path behind the cabin. "Only about fifty feet in the woods, you'll see the platform and a toilet seat chair. "

Though he seemed to be enjoying himself, he mysteriously decided to cut his visit short, and Dick brought him to the Trail several days earlier than planned. I was down on the ice, scooping our daily quota of water, when Dick returned. As he turned off the snowmobile engine, I looked up. "Why is it people have the hardest time with our outhouse and lack of a shower?" I said.

"Don't know," he said. "Maybe we're just slobs—"

"—or living closer to nature," I interrupted. Then another thought struck. "When you think about it, why does an outhouse need walls? It's much nicer without them."

"Don't know." But Dick was already onto a different train of thought. "I checked the mailbox. No job responses."

Drat. I felt a small jolt of worry. Our job search was bogging down. Although we continued to send out résumés, the results had been mixed. A week earlier we'd gotten a response from the University of Minnesota Duluth, where we had sent a résumé for a glassblower position. "Look at this," I cried hopefully when I saw the return address. Opening it, I saw that Dick had been turned down.

Why? Of course there was no answer, but it was acutely disappointing. We liked the North Shore, and Duluth would have been a perfect city.

Hardly better had been the response from Arctic Cat in Thief River Falls. He'd been invited to "stop by" and see them if he was ever in the area. Not much of a proposition.

On the other hand, a medical clinic in southern Minnesota had offered Dick a glassblower proposal. But after reading the letter, his response was: "Not interested."

Several days after Dick's fastidious friend departed, a letter arrived, addressed to me. The vice-principal of the junior high where I had taught informed me of a position teaching seventh grade that was opening the coming year and invited me to contact the principal if I was interested.

I showed it to Dick. "They want me back." I was flattered.

We looked at each other.

"But I don't want to go back," I said.

Dick nodded. "I don't blame you. Don't worry so much. Something will turn up."

I agreed but had my doubts. Would a good job open? I swallowed hard and tried to think positively. "When the right situation comes along we'll know," I said with bravado I didn't feel.

Meanwhile, the task of demolishing the A-frame was almost done. Each morning I trekked down to the A-frame to pull nails and stack lumber while Dick built the new addition and transported useable lumber to our cabin. Nooky was happy trotting from one spot to another.

One morning, I looked up from my task to see the snowmobile barreling down the lake. Dick pulled up with a swoosh of snow. I stopped pulling nails, crowbar in hand. "C'mon down here," He yelled. "Kermit just snowshoed in to the cabin. McGraw Hill in St. Louis called my dad, and he called Loon Lake Lodge. They want me to return the call collect. Get on and let's go."

Throwing down the crowbar, I barreled through the snow and hopped on. We stopped at the cabin to pick up Kermit, and he rode in the sled while Nooky ran alongside as we raced to Loon Lake Lodge.

I waited anxiously as Dick talked on the phone. The coffee Will had given me almost burned my tongue as I swallowed thoughtlessly, too excited to concentrate on anything.

"Good news!" Dick said as he hung up. "This guy likes my

résumé and thinks I'd be perfect for the job. They want me to start as soon as possible..."

That hit like a ton of bricks. "Start now?" I said. A shiver ran through me.

"Yup."

"What's the job?" I was dumbfounded, unable to take it all in.

"Book salesman. They want me to sell books to industrial arts teachers and technical colleges. I'd travel a lot."

This was overwhelming. We'd hoped for a job offer, but this was like a bolt from the blue. I couldn't imagine how we could possibly move from the wilderness to a big city like St. Louis immediately, and the idea of Dick being on the road wasn't sitting well with me either. It was all too sudden. I felt confused and worried. Yet, we'd been hoping for a good job offer, I argued with myself. We needed to think of our future.

Thanking the Johnsons for the use of the phone, we left for home. "Sounds like a good job, good prospects for promotions." Dick said as we walked to the snowmobile. "But the guy I talked to needs to run it through his boss in New York. Then he'll get back to me as soon as he can." He turned to me. "Honey, the salary is really good."

Thoughts bounced around in my head like ping-pong balls. Good money. But long stretches on the road? St. Louis? Perhaps we'd soon have to make some big decisions about our future.

The wait for a reply began.

23

FROZEN MIST

Even as we fretted about our human lives, Mother Nature continued to amaze us. During the last week of February I experienced the most beautiful day of my entire life. Nothing has ever surpassed it.

The previous day had been sleety and dreary, but the sleet froze overnight, creating a shimmering world of ice crystals. When I trudged to the outhouse the next morning, the sun was rising, and as I looked across the lake, the entire south side wore a sparkling, iridescent halo. The sleet had encrusted all the bare branches with a layer of shimmering crystals.

By ten o'clock, I was hard at work on the A-frame while Dick pounded, measured, and cut lumber at the cabin. But I found it hard to keep my mind on the job because every few minutes I stopped to admire the beauty.

Green spruce and pine tree boughs dripped glittering icicles. Bare tree branches sparkled like diamonds against the bright blue of the late winter sky. The best part was the bell-like tinkle of millions of tiny icicles swaying in the gentle breezes that moved through the ice-covered branches.

Again and again, throughout the day, I stopped to drink in

all the beauty, and when the sun set I watched as its last rays lit up the woods with a shimmering radiance, feeling peaceful and thankful for the experience.

❧

There were times when we needed a change from our quiet life on Tucker Lake, and attending the annual Lion's Club Trout Derby was just the ticket. On a warm, sunny March 1, we snowmobiled out to the Trail, hopped in our Bronco, and headed down to the event. When we arrived, the ice-covered surface of Trout Lake was wall-to-wall activity. Dick crept out on the ice, surrounded by people, dogs, and snowmobiles, following one of the plowed "streets" to a good spot on the lake. I'd never been to an ice fishing derby before and bounced on the seat with excitement. "Look at all the people. Why doesn't the ice sink under the weight?"

An ice fishing contest is an remarkable sight to someone experiencing it for the first time. Rows of ice houses (also referred to as ice shacks or ice fishing houses) create avenues and streets on the lake's ice surface resembling a town, and everywhere, the inhabitants of this little town, bundled in snowmobile suits and heavy Sorel or Pak boots, are fishing through holes drilled in the ice, watching their fishing holes, hoping to catch the "big one" that will win the contest. And when they're not diligently fishing, they're whizzing around on snowmobiles.

One of the specialties of this event—provided by its sponsor, the Lion's Club of Grand Marais—is a sandwich of crispy fried herring in a bun. It's called a fishburger, and people line up at the food stand, eager to sink their teeth into this traditional treat. Dogs frolic, tails wagging. Children tumble and chase each other. The colorful display of shiny snowmobiles and people in bright snowmobile suits dazzles against the bright white glare of ice and snow.

After Dick found an open spot, he drilled a hole in the ice

and set a line; then we took turns exploring this "ice city of the north."

My first task was to buy a raffle ticket, hoping to win a snowmobile. We needed a more powerful machine. I crossed my fingers as I headed back to Dick, who was bobbing the line up and down, hoping to lure a large fish to our bait. When I appeared, he handed me the fishing rod.

"I'm starving. I'm going to grab something to eat at the fishburger stand, and then you can get some lunch." He announced, brushing snow off the back of his bib overalls.

"Are you going to try a fishburger?" I said as I took the fishing rod.

"Everyone says they're great."

"They smell kind of fishy to me," I said as he took off with a wave and disappeared into the chattering crowd.

I sat down on the small camp stool we'd had the good sense to bring, settled in, relaxed, and took a look around. It was quite a scene. The crowds were colorful, the snow sparkled brilliant white, the sky was a majestic blue—a perfect day for sitting out on the ice, and I had come prepared to enjoy it, wearing warm chopper mittens and quilted pants and jacket.

When Dick got back, he was munching down the last bite of a fishburger, I handed the line over to him. "Maybe you'll have better luck. I'm getting some lunch."

"Try one of these!" He called, holding up his empty fishburger wrapper. As I ambled slowly over to the food stand, where a line of hungry people had formed, I remained undecided. Dick seemed to have enjoyed his sandwich, and the members of the Grand Marais Lion's Club were certainly proud of their fishburgers, but I hesitated. Could fish ever replace hamburger? When I reached the counter to place my order, I opted for a burger.

I was dousing it with catsup when I suddenly heard my name blared over the loudspeaker. Then I heard a voice calling,

"Joan! Joan!" I looked over to our fishing hole. Dick was thrashing his arms in the air and calling my name.

I ran over to him through the crowd. "What is it?" I was out of breath.

"Your raffle ticket won!"

"What'd I win?"

"Don't know. Get over there and see!'

Arriving breathlessly at a makeshift podium where Lion Club members spent the day announcing fish sizes and awarding raffle prizes, I gasped out my name to an older man wearing the yellow and purple regalia of the club. I knew I hadn't won the snowmobile because it wasn't being raffled until the day's end, so what was I getting?

"Congratulations! You won a snowmobile suit and boots!" To judge from the man's beaming face, he was as thrilled as I was. I couldn't thank him enough and, clutching my prizes, I rushed back to Dick. The prize was easily worth two hundred dollars.

"Look!" I held up the heavy blue snowmobile suit. "It's a Refrigaware," a top-of-the-line brand. "And the boots—real Sorels!" Another expensive item, sturdy and much warmer than my old ones. Dick was delighted.

We weren't as lucky in the fishing department. Although we didn't leave until the sun was setting, we didn't even get a nibble.

The next day we got a different kind of nibble: McGraw Hill got back to us. Dick returned from the mailbox and entered the cabin. "They answered," he announced.

I set down the plate I was drying. His facial expression told me nothing specific, but he wasn't smiling. We'd spent many hours discussing the dilemma caused by an immediate job offer from the publishing company and had decided not to leave Tucker and rearrange our lives any sooner than June. If the company allowed Dick to start work at that point, we'd consider accepting. We hadn't made a final decision, but the money and benefits were tempting.

I watched with mixed feelings as Dick pulled the letter from his jacket pocket. He quietly set it down. "Changed their minds. They aren't interested. Strange…the guy I talked to really liked me, but he had to talk it over with his New York boss. Do you think it's because we live in the woods?" he wondered. "Maybe they think we're weird."

"Could be," I answered, and then added without thinking, "and who cares?" Surprisingly I felt only overwhelming relief, and looking at Dick's face, I realized he felt the same.

"We really didn't want this, did we?" I said.

Our eyes met. Neither of us had wanted this job. In fact, up to this point, none of the job offers we'd gotten had been appealing.

As we stood there, with the March sun high overhead and the rejection letter still in Dick's hands, it struck me: We weren't the same people any more. We didn't want a conventional lifestyle any more than we'd wanted walls around our outhouse. We'd quit our jobs to spend a year in the woods. Why were we even considering walling ourselves in with a conventional lifestyle? Who was I kidding? I didn't want to live in a big city. So why move to St. Louis?

`Our dutiful attempt to plan for our future like "responsible" adults had merely clarified the fact that we loved this part of the world. I could see myself living here. We were meeting new people and becoming part of the community. I'd never planned to live in rural northern Minnesota, but I liked it.

"We need to talk, don't we?" I looked at Dick. Relief spread over his face. "We have to look at our future differently, don't you think?"

Dick opened the fireplace door and threw the letter into the fire, where it disappeared in a poof of smoke. Turning to me, he said, "We need to ask ourselves, could we stay in this remote part of the world from now on?"

I echoed the question. "Could we live in Grand Marais,

250 miles from the Cities, with no family or friends nearby?"

"Staying here would be like jumping off the cliff without a parachute. And it's more than likely we'd have to take low-paying jobs without health care benefits. Could we?"

That last remark stopped me cold. I'd always had some kind of health benefits, even if it had been public health service at the University of Minnesota. It was scary to think of going without. And yet, that might be our only recourse if we stayed in the area. Good-paying jobs with health care weren't easy to come by in these parts.

How crazy could we be? Yet we were both thinking the same thing. Before he went out to find firewood for the night, Dick summed up the conversation. "We'd better start asking locals about jobs."

24

THE TWO-ROOM CASTLE

Dick's thirty-first birthday arrived without fanfare. Though we were busy finishing the addition, I stopped pulling nails and stacking boards at the A-frame early that day to fix a batch of lasagna and bake a yellow cake with chocolate frosting.

We ate a quiet birthday dinner, then listened to the Minnesota state hockey tournament final in which Southwest beat Edina. I had no gift for Dick, but that didn't matter. He told me this entire special year was gift enough.

For the next few days Dick worked like a whirlwind completing the new room. Each morning we woke at daybreak and worked until the sun's last rays. I pried out nails and salvaged lumber at the A-frame while Dick hoisted into place the roof that would cover the new addition, plank by plank. He installed insulation between the rafters and finished a myriad of details. The air over Tucker Lake echoed with pounding hammers.

One morning at breakfast I surveyed the progress Dick had made, hoping fervently that this would be the day he would finish my new kitchen. Crossing my fingers, I asked, "Today?"

He shook his head, "Not sure. Have to see."

I was down on the lake, gathering water from the ice hole, when Dick yelled. "It's time! C'mon up and watch while I open the wall."

Dropping a plastic container onto the ice, I raced up the little hill and into the cabin. From a vantage point near the woodstove, I watched, hoping nothing went wrong. The chainsaw motor echoed from the new room on the other side of the west wall as Dick slowly cut through it. The blade soon appeared through the plywood, slowly and irrevocably slicing a precise doorway in what had until recently been an external wall. When the outline was complete, Dick turned off the chainsaw and carefully removed the cut section to create a handsome opening.

"Here it is," he announced from the far side of hole, gesturing like a musketeer. "Your new kitchen."

I stepped over the threshold, giddy with excitement. "I can't believe it. We've got two rooms...a two-room castle!" I hadn't been this excited in a long time.

"I've still got to finish paneling the ceiling and that one wall," he motioned his head, "but I'll do it another day. Go ahead. Move kitchen stuff in while I set up the table and stove."

I shivered with delight and immediately began lugging plates, coffee cups, frying pans, and silverware from the old room to the new one, oohing and ahhing as I stored them one by one in a rustic knotty pine cabinet that Dick had installed earlier—another donation from Loon Lake Lodge.

"Look at the sun shining in the windows!" I exclaimed. "See how bright and airy the room is. The pine walls and windows make it so light in here."

I set a beige canister decorated with red and green fruit decals next to the stove. I'd purchased it from a Holiday gas station with coupons. "Doesn't this look cheery against the knotty pine?" I gushed. You'd think I'd inherited a Beverly Hills mansion. Truth be told, that's how I felt.

(above) During our stay we turned our one-room abode into a spacious two-room mansion.

(below) The interior of the addition that Dick finished in March. I loved my blue gas stove top, donated to us by Kermit, and I delighted in the cozy look and feel of the room.

When darkness set in, we hadn't finished outfitting the new room, but Dick said, "Let's celebrate anyway. We'll finish tomorrow."

I joined him on the deck as he grilled T-bone steaks over jack pine coals, and we drank champagne left by one of our guests. The March night was unforgettable: sparkling champagne, sizzling steaks, and a thin, bright crescent moon floating in the deep purple of an early spring sky.

I fell asleep that night and dreamt that I was sitting at the new table with my cup of coffee, enjoying the view across Tucker Lake.

~

Within two days we'd finished dismantling the A-frame and were living comfortably in our two-room mansion. It seemed like the height of luxury. But we'd been working hard, and now we took time to play.

"Let's see if we can find that old logging shack I was telling you about," Dick said after breakfast.

"Why not?" I answered. We walked across the lake's hard ice surface to the other side, where we strapped on snowshoes and climbed the same hill where we'd gotten rain-drenched the previous autumn.

"Am I in good shape or what?" I bragged as we reached the top. We slipped and slid down the snowbank leading to the logging road, whooping and laughing until a sudden noise stopped us cold. A roar like a thousand engines filled the air.

"What is that?" I looked overhead for low flying planes.

"It's behind." Dick shouted over the noise, pointing back towards our cabin. "Better get home." We raced downhill to the lake, stumbling in haste.

Breathless and worried, we reached the bottom of the hill, bursting from the trees and out on the shoreline to discover a horde of snowmobiles parked on the lake in front of our cabin.

Dick recognized one of the machines; it belonged to a nearby resort neighbor, and we raced across the lake to greet them.

The resort owners were guiding fifteen snowmobiles and thirty guests on a snowmobile ride and had stopped to show off the local color—us.

First thing I did was start a pot of coffee brewing. Fortunately people either had their own coffee holders or didn't want any, so I managed to satisfy the coffee drinkers. The snowmobilers milled around, socializing with us and one another. Loud bursts of laughter filled the air, accompanied by the roar of machines as the more restless of our guests started swooping in circles or darting across the lake. The group didn't stay long, and soon, thanking us for the hospitality, they all hopped on their sleds and zoomed off down the lake seeking further adventures.

"That was a wild morning." I said, watching the last snowmobile disappear.

"Crazy," Dick answered. "And we didn't find the logging shack either."

"Another day," I said.

25

Brothers and Decisions

"Look." I pointed. "There he is." Lean and lanky, standing out on the lake ice in front of the cabin, duffel bag slung across his back, was my younger brother, Charlie. Grinning from ear to ear, he called out, "Hello!"

He'd written of his plans to visit during the U of M spring break, but as often happens with college students, plans kept changing. We weren't sure if and when he'd appear, but on this Thursday afternoon, we looked out the cabin window, and there he was!

"You found us!" I said, running to hug him. He'd stopped at Loon Lake Lodge for directions, then hiked, following our snowmobile ice trail, until he reached us. I brought him up to the cabin, where we established his personal space—the upper bunk bed.

"We're a little cramped here, so we say 'excuse me' a lot," I told him. "But you know that," I added, remembering that he'd come with us on weekend visits when he was just a high school student.

Charlie adapted easily to our lifestyle, which made for a pleasant visit. The next three days brought tropical fifty-degree temperatures, blue skies, and pine-scented air as tree sap started its spring movement.

If we felt energetic we snowshoed and hiked. At other times, feeling relaxed and mellow, we lounged on the deck in warm sun, listening to Charlie strum his guitar. When the sun set and stars appeared in the pale evening sky, we stayed outside to watch the moon rise.

One evening, after we'd enjoyed the porterhouse steaks Charlie had brought, we bundled up. Dick and I sat on the snowmobile while Charlie stood in the sled, and we raced westward to a rock ledge Dick and I called Turtle Rock. Squadrons of turtles sunned here in the summer.

"You'll love this," I told my brother. "It's got a great view."

Sitting high on thes rocky ridge with a moon approaching full, we were treated to a spectacular view. The moon rose slowly, huge and yellow, gleaming on the white lake's surface and lighting up evergreen tips that spiked the starry sky. An owl hooted once, then fell silent.

"Listen," I told my brother. Cupping my hands, I called "Hallooo…" into the night. Almost instantly, "Hallooo…hallooo" echoed up and down the lake.

Just then, without warning, a red light burst low in the sky onto the eastern horizon. "What's that?" Charlie pointed.

"Don't know," Dick and I answered in unison, our voices troubled.

The red light grew larger and larger, accompanied by increasingly loud noise as it drew closer. We gasped as a jet fighter flew down the length of Tucker Lake at treetop height.

"I swear, if it were daytime, we could have seen the pilot," I commented. (Later in the summer, a jet flew again during the day, and Dick did see the pilot's face.)

"Must be from Duluth's air base," Dick said as the plane disappeared in the west. Our lighthearted mood had vanished, deflated by the intrusion. We tried to recapture our festive mood by shouting echoes again. It worked. Echoes have a way of capturing the imagination, and we spent another hour laughing, talking, and calling echoes from the top of Turtle Rock.

Too soon Charlie's visit came to an end and we snowmobiled him out to the Gunflint Trail, where I watched and fretted as he departed in Dad's car back to Minneapolis.

"I hope he makes it," I sighed. Being eight years older, I still thought of Charlie as my little tow-headed baby brother—a habit I knew I should break.

"He'll be fine," Dick said. "Hop in the car."

We headed north on the Trail to visit Russell and Eve Blankenburg, the people who'd sold us the land on Tucker Lake. They were legendary on the Gunflint Trail, having lived there in the olden days when it was a primitive gravel road into the wilderness. Back then electricity was only a pipe dream.

Greeting us at the door, they hospitably offered coffee. As we settled in for a visit in the living room of their log house, drinking coffee and munching cookies, I looked around, taking in the huge log beams and massive stone fireplace, all local materials. The house was built, for the most part, by Russell and Eve themselves.

I noted the green of the spruce trees outside the window, the sun shining on the melting spring snow, and thought how nice it would be to live like this. The conversation eventually shifted to us and our lives, and soon we were spilling our anxiety at an undecided future.

"We don't want to leave the area and everyone tells us there's work up here, if you're only willing to do it," I said, trying not to sound whiney, "but we haven't found anything."

Russell's next statement completely blew me away. Leaning back in his chair, he looked us both square in the eye and told of an available job on a test drilling rig he was sponsoring right out on the Gunflint Trail that summer. It wasn't that far from our cabin. It was only a summer job, but it was something. If interested, Dick needed to apply to the core-drilling company in Duluth. Russell added that he'd be willing to write a letter of recommendation for him.

I was giddy with excitement but tried to hide my feelings. This might be the opportunity we were looking for, a step we finally could take to stay in the area. We needed to talk. My eyes met Dick's. I got the feeling he felt the same way.

"I appreciate it, Russell," Dick said, "but Joanie and I need to talk it over. We'll let you know as soon as possible."

An hour later, stuffed with cookies and coffee, we said good-bye. My head spun as we hopped in the Bronco. Here was our chance to begin a life in the northland. Could we really do it?

As Dick pulled onto the Gunflint Trail, we started to talk.

"It's our chance…"

"But we'd have no health insurance—"

"No guarantee of making a good income—"

"Far from family—"

"Be like jumping from a plane without a parachute—"

"Who needs a lot of money? Life's been good on Tucker."

"But I don't want to live back in the woods when we have children…"

"We'll move closer to town—"

"I could grow a huge garden…and maybe get some chickens."

"We could build a log house—"

"What if we don't get this job…"

"We'll find another."

We moved from the car to the snowmobile and sped over the lakes, each caught up in our own thoughts, unable to talk over the snowmobile's roar.

The March sun was lowering in the western sky when Dick stopped our machine in front of the cabin. I looked up at our little abode nestled on the small rise under the shadow of the huge white pine and took a deep breath of fresh, crisp air. Nooky raced to the cabin, but I stayed in place.

Dick also stayed seated. We looked at each other, hardly daring to breathe. Finally Dick said, "Let's do it."

"Why not?" I said.

With that, our lives changed again.

26

SNOW AND HEAT

We wasted no time after making our big decision. The next morning, we packed our duffels, locked up the cabin, and headed for Minneapolis to tell our families we'd decided to remain in northern Minnesota permanently.

But first, we drove to the Blankenburgs' log house. No one was home so Dick carefully penned a note and attached it to the doorknob letting Russell know that he was interested in the job and was picking up an employment application at the drilling company in Duluth.

Excited by our new plans, we found the six-hour road trip south to Minneapolis unusually tedious, and we blurted out our news to each set of parents almost as soon as we arrived at their respective homes. In retrospect, I realized that we hadn't given much thought to how they were going to react.

Dad took the news hard. He pulled me aside and asked if we would reconsider for my mother's sake and choose a less remote place to relocate, maybe Duluth. I mentioned this to Mom and she pooh-poohed it. "I never said that. It's Dad. He doesn't want you that far away. I'd love you to live nearby, but it's your life."

It was sweet of Dad, but I took it in stride. He was always very sentimental about his children.

Dick's mother was stoic, but I knew she wanted us closer. Aglow with the excitement of our decision, I had no understanding of how difficult it was for our parents to see us move away until years later when my daughter left for school in San Francisco and my son moved to Utah.

Our friends were also surprised at our decision and said so. "You'll move back," was the prediction we ran into everywhere. We shrugged it off, confident in our choice. "Who cares?" I told Dick. "We're happy."

Elated by our new plans and energized by a Minneapolis spring bursting with pink crabapples and lilacs blooming in profusion, we said good-byes and headed home after a hectic two weeks of visiting and packing, accompanied by two cast-off pieces of furniture from Dick's grandmother—a four-drawer oak dresser and a 1930s metal cabinet painted a sickly green.

What a shock to find Cook County's lakes still covered with ice! Stopping at our mailbox, Dick pulled a letter from the pile that had accumulated during our absence. It was from the drilling company. Once he'd scanned it briefly, he looked up and grinned. "I've been hired to work on the drilling rig," he said. "I start June 15."

Relief flooded over me. Now we had an income until the summer's end. That gave us time to find other jobs and make more definite plans. We'd just have to keep taking things as they came.

We trudged over packed spring snow to the snowmobile in its parking spot behind Loon Lake's old garage. "This might be one of our last snowmobile runs," Dick commented as we transferred Grandma Nelson's cast-off furniture from the Bronco to the snowmobile sled. We strapped both pieces tightly onto the sled with bungee cords, figuring the ride over the ice could be bumpy. Then Dick slowly snowmobiled to our take-off area on

Little Iron. I walked alongside. According to Loon Lake Lodge, the ice was still safe. It hadn't floated yet. If it had, the lakeshore would be separated from the shoreline.

Anxiously I glanced at our loaded-down snowmobile, wondering if it had enough oomph to pull this much weight across the soggy-looking ice, which was covered with glistening puddles and had a grayish, rotten look.

I hopped on the sled, Dick powered up the machine, and with a whump, we hit the ice and sped forward. So far, so good, I said to myself as we moved along.

Suddenly, a large water pool loomed on the ice ahead. I knew conditions could change in a twinkling but this looked disastrous.

"Hang on!" Dick yelled and hit the throttle. We flew forward over the water and had almost reached solid ice again when the snowmobile engine gurgled and we slowed dangerously.

"Keep hanging on!" Dick yelled, his words barely audible over the pounding of my heart. He hit the throttle, and we lurched forward. The momentum kept the sled's runners gliding on ice several inches below the water's surface. When we reached the end of the pool, the sled and snowmobile skated back up out of the meltwater onto solid ice, and I gave a huge sigh of relief.

That was the first of a myriad of melted pools. Each time we went through the same routine. I learned to hop off the sled to lighten the load, and Dick used the same technique of rocketing the snow machine and sled forward through the puddles. By the time we pulled up in front of the cabin, we were experts at the maneuver.

Several hours later, when the sled had been emptied and we'd carried both the dresser and the metal cupboard to the cabin, I sat back and basked in the glory of having two more pieces of furniture. *It's amazing how these two hand-me-downs brighten my world*, I thought.

The dresser was narrow, and we squeezed it into a small space at the base of the bunk beds. The metal cupboard found a home up against the east kitchen wall. As I filled it with Band-Aids, a ball of string, and several pairs of scissors, I vowed that I would paint it a bright color. The pea green simply did not match my rustic décor.

27

BONNIE AND CLYDE

The next morning I woke to cheerful blue skies and the fresh air of Tucker Lake. We were home. Dick had a job. We sat, talked, and relaxed.

Finishing breakfast, I sipped a second cup of coffee and looked out over the lake. "Obviously a job hasn't popped up for me," I said. "But I'll stay home and hold down the fort while you work. Hopefully we'll both get jobs at the end of summer and—"

A clicking noise scrabbled at the small window behind me.

"It's the gray jays!" Dick said, getting up to open the window. Sometime in February, two gray jays had started feasting on tidbits of food we'd thrown out in the dishwater. We named them Bonnie and Clyde and began to feed them regularly. Clyde aggressively grabbed the goodies we offered, even going so far as to feed from an opened palm. Bonnie was less forthright. She always stayed on a nearby branch, polite and quiet, waiting for whatever was thrown in her direction.

Today, Dick threw out a few morsels for Bonnie, then held out a bread crust in his hand for Clyde. Normally the gray bird landed on Dick's palm to take his food, but this morning Clyde bombarded his head with whirring gray wings. "That damned bird is trying to land on my head!" Dick yelled. "We've been feeding him too much."

"Probably," I admitted, thinking of all the extra tidbits I gave him. "Clyde's really gotten nervy lately."

Although Clyde was often rude, this was the first time he was brazen enough to try for Dick's head. "I won't put out any more goodies till this evening," I said, stepping out into the March morning to use the outhouse.

The snow was beginning to melt, and I trod carefully along the slushy path. Suddenly a whoosh of air startled me. Looking up, I saw Clyde diving towards me. I ducked. He flew on by and tried again. This time I flapped my arms at him. "No more food for you," I admonished.

I continued on to the outhouse, but, once again, in a brazen attempt, Clyde tried to land on my head. This time Nooky got involved. She barreled towards the diving bird, barking. Her jaws snapped, but the agile jay merely careened up to escape.

That didn't deter Nooky. She kept a strict vigil for Clyde for the rest of the day. With ears aggressively pasted against her head, she dashed in the gray jay's direction, no matter where he was; perched high on a tree branch or trying to land in the underbrush, it didn't matter to our watchdog. At day's end, Nooky finally stopped guarding and entered the cabin for her evening bowl of kibbles. By then, the deep twilight had forced Clyde back to his night's roost, somewhere in the forest.

❧

Slowly, spring moved northward, and we entered the month of April. The thawing lakes had become useless for travel, and we were forced to walk the mile-and-a-half path we'd made last October from the cabin to the Gunflint Trail. One day Dick stored the snowmobile at Loon Lake and returned home through the woods.

And then, one early April morning, we woke to ten inches of freshly fallen snow. "There goes our trip to Grand Marais," I wailed. I had lots of errands to run.

"Why?" Dick countered. "We'll put on snowshoes. It's not that deep." And that was our introduction to the "in-between" month of April, a limbo where neither a canoe nor a snowmobile could transport us across the lake. Walking through the woods was the only way to reach civilization.

During this season, I watched in fascination as the lake ice slowly melted. First came black, rotten ice, which continued to float as melting water drained from its surface. Today it was entering a new stage: the ice pack was retreating, ringing the entire shoreline with a collar of open water.

An hour later, Dick, Nooky, and I were trudging through the woods. Heavy, wet snow clung to my snowshoes, which made for a strenuous walk. With sweat pouring off my brow, I stopped briefly to catch my breath. Thick snow covered pine boughs, branches, and twigs with glistening white. I was truly walking through a winter wonderland, though as the sun warmed the April morning, clumps of melting snow occasionally fell unexpectedly from tree branches onto our heads and shoulders.

By the time we reached the Trail we were exhausted. But the trip to town was worth it. I was able to buy the latest *Vogue* magazine and also a surprise for Dick. With shopping finished, I stepped into the Bronco and handed him a two-pound box of chocolate-covered cherries. I figured our difficult trek through the woods deserved a reward.

Two days later, the temperatures soared into the 70s, and the heavy snowfall melted almost as swiftly as it had arrived. That evening I leaned back in a deck chair alongside Dick, and we listened to a flock of birds squawk as they circled a huge white pine on the far side of the lake, searching for nighttime roosts. Warm air touched my face, and the setting sun radiated a soft pink.

Nooky sat by my side, nose twitching at scents wafting in on the gentle breezes. She'd brought her pink ladybug out and absently gnawed at it.

Suddenly Dick sat bolt upright. "Look," he said, pointing to the dock. A sleek dark head was surging through the water.

"Beaver," I whispered.

Nooky's nose twitched as she detected the swimming animal's scent, and she moved stealthily down the hill to investigate. The beaver swam steadily east, nearing our log dock just as Nooky hopped onto it. With a mighty whack, the beaver slapped its tail and disappeared.

The splat shocked Nooky, and she raced up the hill, growling all the way, but she liked the excitement. For the rest of the evening her brown eyes searched the lake's surface for another glimpse of the beaver, but the wild creature had chosen a more secluded stretch of shoreline to scavenge for food and building materials, and we didn't see it again.

28

NOOKY AND THE RIVER

As I looked out at the sunny April morning, I knew we'd be forced to spend another day trudging to and from the Trail. A week and a half had passed, and still the lake ice wasn't completely melted.

As I shut the cabin door with an extra tug and followed Dick into the bright day, I was thinking with amazement—though it had happened before—how quickly groceries seemed to disappear, and the dirty clothes pile grew just as rapidly grew. We needed to go to town. It was unavoidable.

Behind the cabin, last night's torrential rain had created a small but fast-flowing run-off. Dick pointed to it. "I'll build a little bridge there tomorrow," he siad. "That spot's always spongy."

I nodded my approval. With the melting snow and the spring rains, the forest was sodden with moisture. The spring melt had made snowshoeing impossible, so we hiked in calf-high rubber boots. Nooky trotted along, often taking detours around puddles and small water sluices. She didn't like getting wet.

Woodpeckers drummed on trees above our heads, yellow and black mourning cloak butterflies flitted through the spring sunshine, and the sound of a male partridge thumping his tail on a fallen tree echoed gently in the distance.

It was a perfect spring day, until we reached the Tucker River.

As we rounded the curve to the hill that led down to the stream, a roaring sound filled the air. "Is that the river?" I gasped, incredulous.

"I hope not," Dick answered as we started down the hill. But the closer we approached, the more difficult it was to escape the realization that last night's heavy downpour had turned the placid Tucker River into a raging torrent.

"Look, Dick!" I pointed to our crossing spot. The rocky stepping stones we normally used were covered with white rushing water. "We can't cross the river. It's too dangerous."

Dick didn't share my fear. "We can get across," he said. I stopped alongside him at the torrent's edge. "Let's figure it out. It's not that deep. See." He plunged his walking stick into the river. I took a close look. The water mark was definitely at a safe level.

"Together, we can lift that log up in the air," he pointed to a dead tree lying near the water, "and let it fall to the other side to make a bridge. Not perfect, and we might get wet if we slip off, but it isn't deep enough to be dangerous."

"I guess so." I wasn't sure I liked this plan. The fast-flowing water, even though shallow, made me nervous, but I couldn't think of another idea except to return to the cabin and wait for the flood to subside. I really didn't want to do that.

"Well, don't stand around! Let's get it done!" He said with more enthusiasm than I felt. I wasn't the only unexcited member of the family. Nooky's brown eyes narrowed in apprehension, and she stayed far away from the water's edge as we lifted, then dropped the dead tree over the torrent. When Dick stepped on the makeshift log bridge, she watched intently as he slowly placed one foot in front of the other and began crossing.

"I'll call her when I reach the shore," he yelled over his shoulder. I watched, with Nooky at my side, wondering if she'd follow him. The surging river frightened me, and I could only imagine how intimidating the rapids would be to a dog.

But I underestimated our dog. Apparently she didn't like being left behind, and as I stepped closer to the river, she darted from behind, passed me, chasing after Dick, and took a running leap onto the log.

I sucked in my breath as she moved across the log, scurrying faster and faster to keep her balance. She'd almost made it across. Her strategy might have worked if Dick had already crossed the log, but he hadn't yet reached the other side. She ran smack dab into him and would have knocked him into the river if he hadn't used his walking stick for balance.

It was poor Nooky who fell into the seething torrent.

And sank. Like a rock. Her black masked face surfaced once before disappearing under the white foaming water.

"Dick!" I screamed. "Do something!" Nooky was pinned on the upstream side of our makeshift log bridge so the current didn't sweep her away, but she was still trapped underwater.

Losing sight of her altogether in the froth, I screamed, "Where is she?" Dick reached into the foaming water, searching for our beloved puppy. I held my breath as his hands grasped for her and came up with empty fists. Nothing but rushing water. He tried again.

This time, he had better luck. "I got her!" he yelled, pulling a handful of fur above the rushing surface. His legs wavered and he almost lost his balance, but he managed to right himself and, holding on for dear life, gave a mighty heave. The sodden Malamute flopped onto shore, looking like a large wet rat.

Immediately she leaped to her feet and ran in manic circles, rolling on the ground to dry her normally fluffy fur.

Dick joined her on the opposite shore. That left me alone on the other side. I carefully crossed, making a concentrated effort to keep my balance while Nooky, her flat, sodden fur making her look half her normal size, continued running in circles.

"You poor thing," I attempted to comfort her once I'd reached shore, but she dodged my sympathy and continued racing back and forth.

We stopped near the river for a few minutes to catch our breath and watch Nooky's antics. "She looked as if she didn't think she'd make it," Dick said, watching her dash about.

"I'm not sure she would have, if you hadn't been there. I think she's just thrilled to be alive." I tried to pet her again but she was too hyper to stop moving, and soon we pushed on while she ran ahead.

As we reached the Trail, an unnerving thought crossed my mind. How were we going to get Nooky to cross the river again on the way home? I shoved the laundry bag into the Bronco and pushed the thought away.

But late in the afternoon, as we returned from town carrying groceries and clean laundry in backpacks, it returned. The closer we got to the river, the louder the sound of rushing water. How would Nooky react to crossing our makeshift log bridge a second time? Would the log even still be there? My stomach felt queasy. When we reached the river the log bridge was still in place, but the rushing water hadn't subdued. It raged, wild and white.

Dick strode toward the bridge and motioned, "Come on, Nooky." He started over the bridge. She stopped, well clear of the gushing water, and looked at him. She wasn't going anywhere.

"C'mon, girl," he sweet-talked, stepping closer to the log. "Be a good girl. C'mon." He patted his knee. Nooky looked at him as if he were crazy and didn't move a muscle. Ears rigid. Eyes mistrusting.

"Nothing to be afraid of," he cooed, his voice dripping honey, as he took a step closer to the river. She sat down a good ten feet away.

I stood between them like some kind of mediator.

Nooky's expression was easy to read. She was not going across that water. Dick gave a heavy sigh. "Okay, I might have to drag you, then." He had to be bluffing. We both knew that wouldn't work.

Still, how else could we get her across? We looked at each other and silently agreed we needed to be more forceful. Nooky seemed to read our minds and moved farther back from the water and away from us. With a sigh, Dick pulled her leash from his backpack and slowly moved towards her, then with a quick motion hooked it up and took a few steps through the mud to the river.

"If I can get her moving, she should be able to run across," Dick said, but he looked nervous. I know I was. I had my doubts. This was going to be a serious test of wills. How in the heck would we convince Nooky to step on the log bridge when she'd almost drowned this morning?

"Come girl!" he wheedled. She dug her rear legs in. He gave another tug, still coaxing. Nooky's whole body tightened, she bent her head and moved steadily backwards, attempting to slither out of her collar.

Dick dropped his hands in frustration and stood with hands on hips. "Not going to cross that river, are you?" he said, leaning over to unhook her leash. She quickly moved out of his reach. She was having none of it.

We looked at each other, exasperated. How could we cope? We had to get her across the river.

I couldn't think of a solution and muttered a silent, irrational word of thanks that the spring days were long, giving us more hours of sunlight to deal with the dilemma.

Suddenly Dick's face brightened. "I've got an idea."

"What?" I couldn't imagine.

I'll carry her," he said. "Piggy-back."

I almost laughed. "She'll never go for it." Nooky weighed a good seventy pounds, but that wasn't the problem. Getting her to jump on Dick's back would be the problem.

"We have to try…" Dick trailed off. "Look. I'll get down on my hands and knees. See if you can get her on my back."

"Okay, but I don't see how this will work."

"Just try it," his voice was edgy. "We have to do something!" He dropped to his hands and knees.

"Okay. I'll give it a try."

Nooky had kept well away from us and the river, but seeing Dick kneeling on the ground brought out the curious side of her nature. If there's one thing a Malamute is, it's inquisitive. She moved one paw a little closer, then the other paw, and slowly, cautiously, approached me. "We're not going to hurt you," I wheedled, and when she got near enough, I gave her a big hug.

While hugging her, I cajoled her onto Dick's back; to my surprise, she cooperated. She wrapped her front legs around his neck. Here's where I give Nooky and her Malamute breed credit for intelligence. I've never been able to explain why she was willing to climb on Dick's back.

But she did.

As he rose from the ground, she grasped him firmly around his waist with her hind legs and, despite all former qualms and frightening experiences, somehow seemed to sense she could trust him to carry her over the fearsome watery maelstrom.

Using his walking stick, Dick stepped gingerly onto our makeshift bridge, and step by step, he carefully crossed the river. I watched nervously, trying not to think of what could happen should she panic and release her grip, yet at the same time I found myself chuckling at the rare sight of a large sled dog riding piggy-back on a man. Nooky clung to Dick's back until they reached solid ground. She never wiggled. She never made a sound. She simply hung on for dear life. As he stepped from the log onto the other shore, she dropped to the ground and once again began to run in ecstatic circles.

I gave a huge sigh of relief, and once I'd made it across the stream myself, Dick and I reveled in our accomplishment, while Nooky frisked back and forth with tail wagging.

29

SUDDENLY IT'S SUMMER

Although the calendar read April 29, the day felt like summer. "I can't believe it's this warm," I told Dick, looking at the thermometer. "It's almost 80!"

He glanced up from the log he was peeling, part of a new deck stairway he was making. "And you're dressed for the occasion."

I'd slipped into shorts and a sleeveless shirt and pulled rubber boots on my feet. "Yep. Going to spade the garden."

I'd read all about organic gardening in *Mother Earth News* and was eager to try it. Local gardeners Eve Blankenburg and Al the Woodsman had suggested I build up the thin soil of the region with organic matter. First, I needed to measure out an area and spade it.

I fancied a spot of land behind the cabin where the sun shone most of the day through the balsam and birch. Plus it didn't seem too rocky.

Pacing out an area that measured fifteen by eighteen feet, I looked at the stones and humus, branches and leaves that needed removal and was glad I'd decided not to go any bigger. Both local garden advisors had recommended I dig down around fifteen inches, sift and remove the rocks and return the remaining soil, then keep adding organic matter. "Anything," Al told me. "Fish guts, coffee grounds, leftover vegetables."

Nooky watched briefly with inquisitive brown eyes, then returned to her favorite spot under the cabin.

I plunged the spade into the soil and pushed down. Clunk. A rock. Remembering the frustration of last autumn's digging experiences, I knew that rocks and stones would plague me, so I gritted my teeth and dealt with it. Pushing from different directions seemed to be the best strategy. The brown humus crumbled and the rock loosened.

The day was sunny and warm, and the scent of pines permeated the air. Birds I'd never heard in Minneapolis sang.

Everything was lovely until a horde of tiny, winged black flies formed a cloud around my head and began to attack. I batted at the swarm. "Phugh!" I spit out several little black critters. Clearing the air around my face, I pushed the spade into the humus and brought up gravel, numerous small rocks, and a smidgen of soil that I carefully deposited on a spot I mentally labeled, "black dirt." Maybe the bugs weren't that bad.

"Ouch!" I was wrong. The black fly horde was growing bigger. Several had infiltrated my socks and were chewing vigorously at my ankles. Another burrowed in behind my right ear. Reaching to scratch it, my fingers grabbed the small body and squashed it.

I stood back for a minute and caught my breath. I'd had plenty of experience with insects on our previous summer visits, but nothing like this. Digging a garden and mucking around in dirt stirred up more swarms than I'd ever thought possible. Swirls of the black pests surrounded me until I actually began inhaling them.

You can't give up. I plunked the spade into the ground, determined not to quit. I lasted thirty minutes (a long thirty minutes) before finally giving up. I glanced at the four square feet of my future garden that I'd dug. It was enough. Setting down the spade, I rushed towards the cabin, swatting at the tormenting insects and swearing.

I slowed down and put on a calm face when I realized I had to get past Dick, who was putting the finishing touches on the new log steps. I had no desire to look like a sissy pants. As I approached, I took a deep breath and acted calm. He was sweeping shavings from the top step. "Nice job," I said. (As with all of Dick's handiwork, the steps *were* well-constructed.)

He stepped back to survey his creation. The stairs did look nice, but now I noticed a problem. With new shiny stairs leading to the deck, the rest of the cabin looked shabby. Dick must have reached same conclusion.

"We need to paint," he said. "The cabin's starting to peel. We should do it before I go to work for the summer, but I don't think we can afford the paint."

I let out a deep breath. I hated to talk about it, but it was true: our funds were running low. I nodded in agreement. The original paint job, which we did in 1966, was now faded, blistering, and peeling. "I don't see how we can afford any paint until you start on the drilling rig."

Between the nasty insects and our dismal money situation, I'd had enough unpleasantness for the day. "We should paint," I agreed, "but right now, I'm heating up some stew," and I climbed the new stairway onto the deck and into the cabin.

Stew always made a satisfying meal. Sometimes I opened a can of Dinty Moore, sometimes I made it from scratch, but we were always hungry and always enjoyed this comfort food. Tonight, I opened a can and heated it. As we filled our bellies with homemade bread slathered with butter and dipped in the beef, vegetables, and gravy, we discussed our biggest problem: money.

This year's adventure had changed our lives for the better and made us realize we didn't want money to be its main focus. On the other hand, you can't live on love alone. Our savings, which originally amounted to $1,100, were disappearing as fast as the ice on Tucker Lake.

"It's going to be tough making money last until I start the drilling job. That's six weeks away." Dick lifted a gravy-soaked piece of bread to his mouth.

I agreed. "If there was just some way to bring in even a little until then..." I trailed off. We'd heard of day jobs that were available—clearing brush, handy-man tasks—but so far nothing even remotely practical had turned up. They'd all been located on the other end of the county. Not worth the gas money.

"Nothing to do but tighten our belts," I said.

"And keep baking bread," Dick added.

We lapsed into silence, each pondering our own impractical schemes and flights of fancy. In the end, all we could do was hope that something would turn up. We just had to be patient. I stood up and began clearing the table.

After washing dishes, we covered ourselves with bug dope, carried our coffee mugs to the deck, and watched the spring evening unfold. A noisy flock of crows lit in the tall pine on the island across the lake, their squawky but cheerful gabble filling the otherwise quiet evening. We watched as the sun set in pale shades of rose.

"Look!" I pointed to the opposite shore. Something dark was moving across a large patch of splotchy ice. Looking closer, I saw it had a shiny brown coat. A beaver! As we watched, it slid over the frozen surface, found open water, and disappeared with a slap of its tail.

As we watched the tranquil pink sky catch the last rays of the sun, I said, "I'm still happy we decided to stay up here. Comes at a price though, doesn't it?"

Dick nodded.

Eventually the mosquitoes, even with all our bug dope, forced us inside. As I brushed my teeth, I noticed the area around my right eye was swollen and starting to sting. When

I showed Dick the welt, he said, "black fly bite" matter-of-factly.

Next trip to town, I bought a mosquito netting hat and thereafter wore it when working in my garden. And I never gardened in shorts again.

30

THE ICE IS OUT!

With a soft breeze at our backs, we steered the canoe toward the landing on Little Iron. I looked up at the blue sky and gentle waves and smiled. After seven months, we were finally on open water. Morning clouds had scudded away. Bright sunlight and 70-degree temperatures filled the day.

A warm but fierce wind had blown all yesterday and broke up the blackish and rotten lake ice. Not having finished the job, the wind next forced the ice chunks to the middle of Tucker, where they slowly dissipated in the warm afternoon sun. By early evening only a few lonely icebergs remained. The next morning when I looked out the front window, they had all disappeared.

The first thing Dick and I did was hop in the canoe and head for the Gunflint Trail. "No more hiking through the woods with those damn heavy backpacks," I gloated as the four-horsepower motor pushed the canoe down the lake. "We can float in our little canoe."

As a warm May breeze riffled my hair, I mentally went over today's schedule. We needed to visit the Blankenburgs and check the mail, but the main reason we were out and about was to enjoy the spring air. We'd also decided that moving the

Bronco from its winter location to a summer spot closer to the canoe portage was a good idea.

After pulling our boat ashore on Little Iron, we followed the short path to the Gunflint Trail. Tiny green leaves peeked out from the forest floor. A partridge drummed. I stopped and listened to the long, sweet descending song of white-throated sparrows as they whistled in the distance. I felt marvelous.

When we reached the car, we found a note stuck under the windshield wiper.

"What? What is it?" My excitement morphed into worry as Dick read it without expression. It could be good or bad news. He wasn't showing any emotion until he finally looked up and cracked a huge grin. "Some guy wants me to work clearing his lot on Loon Lake. He's putting up a cabin. It means money, honey!"

I almost did a happy dance but decided to act with decorum—though inside I was dancing a jig.

"He left a phone number," Dick said. "We'll call him from Loon Lake Lodge after we visit the Blankenburgs. We should see them first."

But the day got complicated. When we arrived at the Blankenburgs' place, Eve informed us that Russell was sick, so we cut our stay short.

We hadn't taken the time to check our mailbox for last week's mail, figuring we'd wait until today's mail had arrived and pick it all up at once. When we returned from our visit to the Blankenburgs, we finally took a large batch of mail from the box. Dick opened a letter from his mother and was completely surprised by her news. Dick's Grandpa Nelson had died on April 30, and the funeral was today. Grandpa Nelson was actually Dick's step-grandfather, who loved to delight Dick by wiggling his large ears.

"I should have picked up the mail Saturday." Dick's face was somber.

"There's no way you could have known." I consoled him. "We only check mail every other day."

"Still, I'll call the folks anyway."

The Johnsons were busy moving from The Shack and getting the lodge ready for opening fishing, but as always, they welcomed our use of their phone.

In The Shack, I waited as Dick called his parents, watching as his furrowed brow cleared and relief filled his eyes. He hung up the receiver. "Mom said she and Dad didn't expect us to make it to Grandpa's funeral. There's nothing we could do about it and not to worry. What's done is done."

But some of the day's bright happiness dimmed as I realized I'd never see Grandpa Nelson or his wiggling ears again, and although Dick didn't say anything more, an occasional shadow passed his face, and I knew he was thinking of his grandfather.

≈

The sun rose in the sky, the day moved on, and we now needed to deal with the guy interested in hiring Dick for the day job. Once again, Loon Lake Lodge encouraged us to use their phone. Dick dialed the number left on the note but got no answer. Answering machines were still a thing of the future, so we were forced to dally around at the lodge for several hours while we tried to reach the man. No luck.

I felt like knocking my head on one of the huge cabin logs. We really needed that job. The money would tide us over to Dick's drilling rig job. I was seething with frustration. We needed to find out about the job and needed to find out now.

Finally, Kermit saved the day. "Here," he said, handing Dick a postcard. "Write a note, tell him you'll take the job for three dollars an hour. The mailman will pick it up tomorrow."

It was the perfect solution. Later, as Dick set the postcard in the mailbox and turned the flag to an up position for the postman, he said, "Maybe I asked for too much. Maybe I should change it."

Kermit, who'd come with us to the mailboxes, said, "Don't. That's the going rate. You should get paid that much."

So leaving the card as written, we said good-bye to Kermit and walked to our boat landing on Little Iron. "I don't know," Dick said as we climbed into the canoe. "Maybe we're asking for too much money."

"Maybe," I said, "but Kermit knows the going rate, and three dollars an hour could amount to twenty-four dollars a day. That would pay for two weeks' worth of groceries."

31

Gardening Is a Lot of Work

It was a sunny day in late May. Spring had turned to summer. After a long winter and a highly variable spring, warm temperatures were finally here to stay, and this made it possible to leave winter survival mode behind for good and devise a new summer regime. Top on my list was my garden.

It was tidy and neat, but after I'd rooted out the rocks and grit, there wasn't much soil left, and it clearly needed enrichment. Being young and idealistic, I wanted to be completely organic, and every day, with a zealot's fervor, I buried coffee grounds, eggshells, and leftover veggies in the thin, unsubstantial dirt. But it wasn't enough.

Then Dick had a brainstorm. He suggested we take a walk down our Tucker River path to see if we could find some completely natural fertilizer. "I've seen lots of moose crap in that area," he said. "And it's free."

Before long we came upon a large pile of shiny brown moose droppings spilling over the sides of the path. "They're beautiful!" I squealed as I knelt to scoop the pellets into a plastic bag with a garden trowel.

"I told you we'd find a bunch here," Dick said.

"This is fantastic!" I rapidly shoveled as many of the impressive brown pellets as I could fit on my small scooper into the bag while Dick walked ahead searching out more.

We were fertilizer hunting.

A soft breeze touched the back of my bug-repellent-covered neck. Flying insects by the gazillions were the only negative part of summer in the woods.

"Found more!" Dick yelled from the path ahead, and, scooping up a final turd, I trotted over to him. I didn't want to miss a single bit of this great natural nitrogen.

Dick pointed. "Bonanza!" I yipped as I dug into this new pile. Moose droppings were the tidiest form of wild animal fertilizer I could think of. Shaped like large, smooth peanuts and quite dry, the droppings were easy to harvest.

"I'm counting on fresh garden peas and sweet corn," Dick said. "That's part of my finder's fee."

"Don't worry. You'll have a feast," I assured him, "but you'll have to wait till August."

"I'm looking forward to it!" Dick said. "Let's see if there's more this way." He followed an opening in the birch trees—it seemed logical that moose would walk that way—and I followed behind with my pooper scooper.

Yes, I had high hopes for my garden. No seeds planted yet, but I'd dug up all the humus, screened it for rocks and gravel, and then put it back on the ground. True, the amount of humus I'd come up with was less than I'd hoped, which made the area I'd dug up area looked like a sunken garden, but that's where the organic matter came into play. I planned to throw anything I found into the garden.

I spent the next two days alone, while Dick helped clear property over on Loon Lake for the future cabin owner. With Nooky as my faithful companion and guard dog, I filled the long hours baking bread, fishing along the cabin's shoreline, and searching for strawberries. Loneliness never occurred to me.

Dick returned with cash on the second day, along with some exciting news.

"I stopped on the portage, checked out all that black muck, and it looks good for garden soil. Got lots of earthworms…"

"Great." I'd read that earthworms were an excellent addition to soil. They aerated and fertilized at the same time. "Good project?"

"You bet." Dick sniffed the air. "Homemade bread?"

"And canned chicken over boiled potatoes." It was an uninspired meal, but we hadn't been to town that week, and without refrigeration, my menu options were limited, though I fantasized that within weeks my garden would be supplying us with lettuce, green onions, baby carrots. All I had to do was find a little more soil and plant the seeds.

Dick must have read my mind. "Let's go to the portage after we eat and dig up a couple of plastic garbage cans of that black dirt."

After supper, we slipped on our rubber boots, armed ourselves with insect repellent, and canoed to the portage, leaving Nooky behind to guard the cabin.

Under the evening sun, with clouds of insects filling the air around our mosquito net–covered heads, we shoveled muck until the cans were full, then carefully loaded them into the canoe and chugged home down the lake.

Dark was setting in by the time we got back, so we placed the soil-filled containers behind the cabin beside my dug-out garden area, ready to be dealt with in the morning.

Hot, sweaty, and tired, we brushed our teeth and went to bed. Although it was sweltering in the cabin that night, and a small flock of rogue mosquitoes hummed and roamed through the hot, still air, the exercise had exhausted us and we slept like babies.

The next morning broke hot with the potential of being a scorcher. Groggy with sleep, I filled the coffee pot and was slicing bread when Dick came inside from his morning bathroom visit.

His face wore that funny expression that meant trouble. "You're not going to believe this." He stood by the door. "Come and take a look."

"What is it?" Still half asleep, I didn't want to be bothered.

"Just look," he insisted.

With a dramatic sigh, I followed him out the door, around the cabin to the garden.

"What—? What happened?"

The two garbage cans of black soil were upside down.. We looked at each other and simultaneously said, "bear." Nothing else could have turned over those heavy containers.

But I was puzzled. "How could we not have heard it? And why didn't Nooky bark?" I glared at her. She was sniffing the garbage can lid strewn on the ground.

Dick inspected the dirt we'd transported from the portage. "Here's the kicker," he said. "All the earthworms are gone!"

I prodded the black soil with a stick. No worms. Not a single angleworm. "Drat. I really wanted those critters working my soil."

"Too late," Dick said. "They were a bear's midnight snack."

"I still can't believe we didn't hear it," I said as we trudged back to the cabin. "And you should be ashamed." I pointed at Nooky.

She had the grace to look embarrassed.

32

SUMMER ALONE

The sun had barely risen in a pale sky and gray wisps of mist floated over the water as Dick, wearing a long-sleeve shirt and with rain gear in tow, pushed the canoe away from the dock and headed for the Gunflint Trail and his new job.

It was five o'clock in the morning, and weather forecasters predicted a hot day. I stood on shore and waved until the canoe disappeared around the point. It was June 10, 1970: the day our freedom ended.

I looked down at Nooky.

"Just you and me now," I said. Her brown eyes gazed up, her tail wagged, and she moved towards the cabin, breakfast on her mind.

The day stretched endlessly ahead. Dick hadn't been given his schedule so I had no idea how long I'd be alone. Deciding to go with the flow, I stumbled back to the cabin, feeling groggy despite a cup of strong coffee. I poured a second cup and planned my day.

The first task I assigned myself was to set up a batch of sourdough bread, which would rise on the still-warm woodstove top. I was amazed that nights were often still cool enough to warrant a fire in the stove, yet daytime temperatures could soar into the 80s.

Next, my garden. Remembering how my mother planted straight rows by tying a string to a stake at each end, I found an old ball of twine in Dick's jumble pile, broke off two small tree branches, and followed her example.

My little garden seemed to shrink among the tall forest trees as I looked for more space in which to plant all the veggies I desired—carrots, green lettuce, radishes, sweet corn, green beans, cantaloupes, and butternut squash, which wouldn't be ripe until autumn.

The green beans took up the last remaining space, and I realized my dreams were bigger than my garden dimensions. Taking off the red bandana covering my head, I wiped beads of sweat from my brow. I wasn't in the mood to dig and sift more soil, so I'd have to give up the winter squash and cantaloupe. I half-convinced myself that these two would never ripen anyway in the northland's short summers. Sour grapes, anyone?

"See, Nooky," I called her to my side as I finished patting the earth over the last bean seed. "I've finished." She wagged her tail politely—she wasn't much for gardening—and returned to her burrow under the cabin and her beloved toy ladybug. Ensconced in her favorite lounging spot and invisible except for her black nose, she was nonetheless a serious watchdog, keeping a tight vigil over her territory, always barking at any unusual happening. I could count on her to let me know if a fishing party was nearing the cabin, or if a moose was tramping through the woods.

From that first day alone to the last, I never once felt fear with her at my side.

By nine o'clock, my garden was planted and the bread dough had risen into a glistening white mound. I shaped two loaves, put them in pans, and flattened out the remaining dough, sprinkling it with cinnamon and sugar and rolling it into a long tube that I sliced into generous cinnamon rolls.

Even though the weather forecast was for warm temperatures, I stoked up the wood stove and had finished baking the bread and rolls by noon.

Painting the deck took another two hours. I rounded out the afternoon by casting for walleyes off the dock, sunbathing, and, in late afternoon, prepping the evening meal. Today it was leftover meatloaf sandwiches.

Nooky and I started watching for Dick around five. I opened a book and we sat on the deck as a small breeze ruffled the waters of the lake. Dick had been gone for twelve hours. We waited. Five thirty rolled by, then five forty-five, six o'clock. I was a little worried but shrugged it off. Dick had warned me he could be late, and the sun didn't set till at least nine. He'd show up, I assured Nooky. She didn't look worried.

At seven o'clock, the canoe finally rounded the bend as Dick pushed the motor to its max. His shoulders sagged with exhaustion as he pulled up to the log dock.

"Whew," he said as he landed and pushed himself up out of the canoe. "That's a long day. They've got us working eleven-hour days. But the bonus is..." he shouldered his backpack and started up to the cabin, "every other weekend is a long one—four days."

"Sounds great, if you can take it." I led the way into the cabin and set out plates of meatloaf sandwich and fried potatoes. As Dick washed his hands, I asked, "How did the day go?"

"Good." He sat down and picked up his sandwich. "Fred is a really nice guy. Today we set up the rig, and tomorrow we start drilling. It's a long day, though." He gobbled his meal in silence with the appetite of a man who had worked hard.

"Sure am tired," was his only comment as we finished eating and moved to the deck for after-dinner coffee.

"My day was quiet, but not bad." I started telling of my gardening achievement, but when I looked over at Dick, he was almost asleep in his chair.

"Let's go to bed early," I suggested. "We've got to get up at the crack of dawn."

33

LAZY HAZY CRAZY DAYS OF SUMMER

We'd settled into the new routine. Dick worked and commuted a daily six-mile round-trip by canoe. Working eleven-hour days, coming home late, and rising at four thirty in the morning was never easy, but he managed. His got his reward during those wonderfully long four-day weekends.

Once a week, I joined Dick on his early morning commute to the Gunflint Trail where our vehicle was parked. I took the car and dropped him off at the driveway to a nearby lodge, and his co-worker gave him a ride to the drilling rig site. Meanwhile, I drove the forty miles to Grand Marais, where I spent the day buying groceries, doing laundry, and running errands.

This small town has a harbor, a lighthouse, several rocky beaches, and a few streets lined with shops. In some ways it resembles a New England fishing village. I would spend my first two hours at Sjoberg's laundromat. By the time the laundry was dried and I'd folded it back into our duffel bag, the other stores would be open.

On this occasion I shopped for new sandals at Joynes Ben Franklin and magazines at Leng's Fountain. I bought gas, went to the library, and explored areas I'd never visited before.

Croftville, three miles east of town, with its cabins clinging to the rocky Lake Superior shoreline, was fascinating, and a few miles west of town, I enjoyed sitting at the Cut Face Creek overlook with its panoramic view of Grand Marais and Lake Superior. I checked out books in the library and bought lunch at the A&W, but by midafternoon time had begun to hang heavy. All in all, I was hugely relieved when four o'clock rolled around, and I could head back up the Trail with a cooler full of cold beer, chicken, and steak to pick up Dick. With no refrigerator, cold beverages and fresh meats were relished treats that in summer had to be consumed immediately.

Following our usual canoe and portage routine, we finally got home. Dick pulled the canoe up in front of the cabin, the bow touched the dock, and as I bent over to tie the line, Nooky leaped out. I caught a glimpse of her flattened ears as she raced up the cabin path barking furiously and disappeared into the woods.

"What the—!" Dick exclaimed.

"Nooky!" I screamed. "Come back!"

Only two animals could cause such a reaction—a bear or a moose. Tangling with either one was to be avoided. Heart pounding, I jumped out of the canoe; Dick followed, and we ran behind the cabin. There was nothing there, so we ran farther, pushing through the underbrush past the outhouse. Nooky's barks took on a higher pitch, but we couldn't see her. "Where is she?" Dick was perplexed. "What's going on?"

Panic overtook me. Then—a new noise. A snort.

"That's not Nooky," I said.

Another snort. We clambered through the woods, desperate to know her whereabouts. Finally, "There she is!" Dick pointed. I caught a glimpse of Nooky's tan fur moving along the shoreline about a hundred feet away. No sooner had I caught a glimpse than she disappeared. Her barking rose to a new level. We moved forward, following the sound, still not seeing her.

Bushwhacking through the thick brush was difficult. Dick moved slightly ahead and finally got a better look at what was going on. "She's barking at something in the lake," he said. "Stay here and keep an eye on her." He turned and ran past me, heading back towards the cabin. "I'll take the canoe out and see what's happening."

He disappeared, and I found myself alone. If the noise was a mother bear protecting her cubs, things could get very tricky. I couldn't see through the brush, and though I wanted to be closer to what was happening, I didn't want to exacerbate the situation, so I stayed put.

The barking continued; occasionally Nooky's pitch would rise. At other times I could hear her growling, low in her throat. The snorts didn't stop either, sometimes louder, sometimes softer. I was ready for anything.

The wait seemed endless until I heard the rumble of our outboard motor out on the lake. Then I heard Dick's voice: "Come on Nooky…come on."

What was happening? I listened, holding my breath.

The barking stopped, and so did the snorting, but that told me nothing. Should I yell, or would that startle whatever critter was out there?

Dick's voice finally called from the lake. "Joanie. It's okay Don't worry. It's all clear. It's a moose and her calf. They're moving down the shoreline away from you."

"Good!" I shouted, and, feeling a huge weight lift from my shoulders, I ran back to the cabin and down to the dock. Circling for a landing, Dick, with a proud-looking Nooky, floated in.

"What happened?" I said as he threw me the rope and I tied up the canoe. Nooky, looking like the cat that swallowed the canary, leapt out, tail wagging.

"She trapped a mama moose and her calf in the lake," he said, jumping out. "They must have been somewhere behind the cabin when we pulled up, and Nooky took off after them.

With a little one to protect, Mama went into the lake to escape Nooky, then charged, trying to scare her off."

I finally understood. "So Nooky charged back from the shore."

"Guess so," Dick said. "At any rate, the water's too cold for a baby moose, so I got the canoe between the moose and Nooky, and when I touched shore, Nooky was very happy to jump in and be rescued."

When everything finally settled down, we celebrated Nooky's accomplishment with cold beer and perfectly grilled steaks. Nooky continued to reign as our supreme watchdog, although she was hoarse all the next day and kept her barking to a minimum.

34

WOODLAND ENCOUNTERS

June's long, sunlit days flew by as we adapted to Dick's brutal new work schedule. Although he invariably returned exhausted, Mother Nature often rewarded him with wildlife displays.

"You'll never guess what happened today," he said one evening as he climbed from the canoe after another long day.

"You saw another moose?" I guessed, walking alongside him as Nooky circled, tail wagging. (He'd spied a cow moose with twin calves near the portage the previous day, the mother looking like a huge and comical horse, the two little ones stumbling to keep up with her on their long gawky legs.

"No," he said. "Guess again." I gave it some thought. Several mornings ago as he waited by our mailbox for a ride from his co-worker, a bear had popped out of the woods. Ignoring Dick, who had decided to wait in our car to avoid the mosquitoes, it went over to rummage in Loon Lake Lodge's nearby garbage can, tearing open bags and filling its belly with gusto. Dick had a comfortable ringside seat from which to watch the great black creature. Occasionally the bear glanced in his direction, but it was more interested in food than in Dick. Finally, Bumper, the resort's resident collie, hurtled towards the bear, barking furiously, which sent the wild creature scurrying off into the woods.

"Another bear?"

"One more guess," Dick said.

"Oh come on." I was getting slightly exasperated. "Another partridge and chicks?" (One evening as Dick crossed the portage, a hen partridge had hopped out onto the path, then moved away, dragging a wing. As he watched, the soft peeps of chicks under the thimbleberry leaves caught his attention, and he stepped off the path to find them. Seven little fluff balls popped into view, all peeping for their mother. The mother immediately stopped her "broken wing" act and flew at him, hissing. Dick got the message and returned to the path, while the protective mother and her little brood disappeared down the portage path, moving at great speed.)

That wasn't it either.

He finally told his story.

This morning had been a hot one, and as he worked on the drilling rig, his throat became parched, so he decided to get a drink. He strolled towards the water pump and absent-mindedly knocked on the fender of the Bronco as he passed. Something knocked back.

He stopped dead in his tracks.

What could possibly be under the hood of his car? Dick was flummoxed. Curiosity overwhelmed him, and, figuring whatever it was couldn't be large enough to be dangerous, he decided to take a look.

He slowly lifted the hood, bent over to stare into the engine compartment, and found himself nose to nose with the startled round face of a woodchuck. Dick jumped back, and so did the little brown creature.

They stared at each other for a few seconds, then Dick slowly closed the hood. "I decided to leave well enough alone."

When he got back to the rig, he was still shaking his head

in amusement, and his co-worker asked, "Something wrong?"

"You'll never guess what I found under the hood of my car," Dick said. "A woodchuck sitting in my engine compartment!"

The two men shared a good belly laugh and returned to their chores.

Within half an hour, they doubled over with laughter again when the same little woodchuck popped out from the under-brush into the clearing and glanced around with a shocked look as if to say, "Oh no! I'm in the wrong place again," and disappeared again into the woods.

When Dick finished his story, I made a confession, "I know your days are long and exhausting, but I'm jealous of all your wildlife adventures."

That night Dick ate with gusto the meal of sloppy joes I'd prepared and was asleep within an hour.

35

LONG WEEKENDS AND THUNDERSTORMS

The scratching at the cabin door caught my attention, and setting down my copy of *Diary of a Mad Housewife*, I went over to open it. As Nooky scurried in, ladybug in mouth, I was surprised to see raindrops.

"What's the matter with you?" I asked as she darted past me. "You don't mind a few raindrops, do you?"

The distant rumble of thunder answered my question. "Bad storm coming?" I asked, hoping her uncanny ability to predict storms was wrong. She heard thunder long before Dick and I did and quaked with fear even when far-off lightning lit the sky.

She scurried under the bed and peered out anxiously, her ears cocked. Another boom of thunder crashed, closer this time, and her furry body shook. I reached down and scratched under her collar, hoping the storm would be brief.

Glancing at the clock, I realized Dick would be home soon. I should have been cooking, but I didn't want to stop comforting Nooky, so I decided to simplify the evening meal plan and open a can of soup. I continued scratching Nooky, but every flash of light, every rumble of thunder, started her quaking again.

Suddenly an immense boom shook the small cabin, followed by a blinding white blast of lightning. Nooky scrabbled as far under the bunk as possible. This was going to be a bad one.

Dick should be somewhere between home and the Gunflint Trail, and I was worried. But he knew better than to venture out on a lake when bad weather threatened. He'd promised he would hunker down somewhere and wait out storms if necessary.

Nooky slowly moved next to me, her body quivering. I hugged her. "It's okay, big girl," I sweet-talked. "You'll be fine." She didn't stop trembling, and another crash of thunder sent her back under the bed.

As the minutes ticked by, the storm increased. Intense gusts of wind screamed past the window. Long blue-white lightning strikes filled the sky—at the same time beautiful and frightening—and the thunder crashed in deep, turbulent waves. No wonder Nooky was terrified.

There was nothing I could do but wait it out and comfort Nooky.

Finally the roiling thunder began to soften, leaving peaceful intervals that sounded like silence, though the rain was still coming down. The lightning strikes became more distant, less threatening, and the gusts of wind less violent. I breathed a sigh of relief as the storm's fury seeped away.

Rain still fell softly. Eventually I poked my head out the door and inhaled the fresh cool air. Dick was probably venturing out now that the lightning strikes had moved off toward the horizon. Nooky quietly padded to my side. She was no longer shaking. She glanced at her food dish. Good. The worst was over. She wouldn't be relaxed enough to eat if her keen ears had detected more stormy weather approaching.

Twenty minutes later, Dick pulled the canoe up to the dock. "That was a pip!" he commented, coming through the door. Nooky, who'd gone back to her burrow under the cabin, followed him in.

"Where did you stay?" I asked.

"The portage," he said. "I hunkered down. That storm came up fast."

"I'm glad you're home safe and sound." I ladled soup into a cup, and added, "You should have brought Nooky along. She predicted it was coming before it was here."

The next morning—the first day of Dick's long weekend—dawned hot and sunny. These weekends were wonderful, something to look forward to during the extended stretch of work days. We relaxed on long weekends, making no plans, doing whatever felt good. "Do we want to go to town or go fishing?" I asked as we sat at the kitchen table, looking at the shimmery summer lake.

"Town." Dick answered. "Stop at A&W, get some burgers, and look around. See what kind of town we're moving to."

We were happy to be staying in this beautiful country, although uncertain about where we'd find work once the drilling job ended. We knew Dick would be able to find manual labor, and we'd have to live wherever that took us. It could mean staying on the Gunflint Trail, or moving east towards Hovland and the Canadian border, or west as far as Taconite Harbor, or staying put in Grand Marais.

Dick could always find a job. The same wasn't true for me. I had no illusions about the difficulties of getting hired in a small-town school district. I'd applied, but nothing had materialized. A librarian's assistant job had been filled before I could even apply. It was disappointing, but I'd cope.

I brightened when Dick suggested we head into town. I often went alone, but on those trips I never went anywhere other than laundromat, grocery store, and library. It'd be fun to scope out the area with Dick, and also to see everything with the fresh eyes of prospective residents.

With Nooky sitting between us, we spent the day driving around Grand Marais and the nearby backroads. We drove through neighborhoods perched on the shores of Lake Superior and critiqued their fantastic views. When we passed lovely houses in the backwoods, we discussed the merits of living in the woods. We had already carried on long conversations across the kitchen table about what kind of house we'd build for ourselves someday—backwoods, town, or lakeside. When Dick turned up the Gunflint Trail, my head was swimming with a myriad of future opportunities.

We didn't get back to the cabin until eight in the evening, just as the sun was lowering. As daylight lingered, we sat on the deck another hour and watched the sun toss delicate shades of pink across the sky. It was a perfect ending to the first day of Dick's long weekend, with three more peaceful days ahead.

36

TURTLES EVERYWHERE

A rustling noise in the underbrush nearby grabbed my attention, and I stopped spreading coffee grounds in the garden. Something was moving under the leaves, not fifteen feet away.

Slowly and stealthily I set down my mulch bucket and tiptoed closer to the noise. What could it be? Since it was hidden by underbrush, it couldn't be very big. Another swish and a small patch of shiny green caught my eye. Looking closer, I glimpsed two reptilian feet. It was a turtle. More accurately, it was the rear end of a turtle scuttling out of sight.

"I didn't know turtles could move that fast!"

"What did you say?" Dick called from inside the cabin. Another long work week had passed, and he was enjoying his day off.

More rustling caught my attention, and I spotted another turtle scampering up the hill at an impressive clip.

"Come on out here!" I yelled. "You've got to see this."

"Okay. Okay." The cabin door shut with a bang and Dick appeared at my side. "What's going on?"

"Turtles." I said. "They're everywhere. They're all over the place! Well, at least two of them are. What are they doing here?"

"Look." Dick pointed to the lake. Another turtle circled the waters around our dock.

"We're being invaded by turtles!" I said. "Why?"

"Maybe egg-laying time?" Dick guessed. Occasionally we spotted turtles sunning on the large rock ledge on the west end of the lake, but I didn't remember seeing them elsewhere. Now they seemed to be flocking to the small hill that rose from the lake in front of our cabin.

"Let's follow one," I suggested. "See if it lays eggs."

"We'd better hustle," Dick said. "They're moving a lot faster than I thought they could."

"Afraid a turtle will outrun you?" I taunted. "Come on." I took off through the underbrush.

"Don't be ridiculous." He moved in the opposite direction so we could cover more ground. I walked a loose grid, intent on finding turtles.

"I'll cover the area on the other side of the little bridge," Dick said, referring to the plank walkway he'd built for the spring run-off. "You'd think they'd be in this boggy area, but I don't see or hear any," he added. "The solstice will be in a couple of days. Makes sense they'd lay eggs now."

"True," I said—though it made no sense to me—and we kept searching. During the twenty minutes we spent sneaking through the underbrush, I spotted only one more turtle, and it disappeared in a flash. Dick and I were reaching the same conclusion. The turtles didn't want to be seen.

We were about to give up our quest when a noise rang through the quiet air. "Halloo!"

"What was that?" Dick asked.

"Halloo." Our heads swiveled. It was a voice down on the lake.

"Company." I pointed.

Giving up our turtle search, we trotted down to the lake just as two boats carrying two young men and five children pulled up to our dock.

"We're with the group camping on the islands," one of the men said.

We nodded. We'd seen their pitched tents and heard children's voices.

"You guys need help with something?" Dick asked.

"Oh no." The other man laughed. "We're fine, but the kids noticed your dog and asked if they could see it. Do you mind?" People were often smitten with Nooky's big brown eyes and her soft and beautiful tan fur.

"Go ahead," Dick said. Chattering and squealing, the youngsters, who ranged in age from four to twelve, jumped ashore. Nooky loved people, and unleashing her charms, she allowed the children to pet, scratch, and make a fuss over her as she rolled and romped with them like an adorable furball.

Dick and I chatted with the men about fishing and the weather until the children got bored. By that time Nooky had also had enough, and her fluffy tail disappeared under the cabin. As everyone piled back into the boat, the man we'd spoken to first cleared his throat. Something about his demeanor caught my attention. I looked up. "I hope you don't mind if I have an unusual request," he said.

I nodded. *What on earth could he possibly want?*

"If your dog ever mates with a wolf," he said, "I'd love to buy a puppy."

That idea did not make me happy, and before Dick could answer, I gave my two cents worth. "We do everything we can to avoid that."

He was undaunted. "Well, in case that somehow happens, would you mind if I leave you my name and address so you can contact me?"

"It's really dangerous for the dog, you know," I started off, and was about to launch into a lecture, when Dick flashed me a look that said, "Just let it go." I suppressed my feelings as I held out my hand to take the man's name and address, which he'd scribbled on a slip of paper. He seemed delighted. No need to tell him I'd be ripping it up the minute he was out of sight.

"Thanks!" he said. As the boats sped away, the children's cries of "Good-bye, Nooky" echoed in the distance.

Dick turned to me with a determined look. "I'll make sure Nooky will never get close enough to a wolf for that to happen," he said.

"Just like we did last winter," I agreed and added. "What's with these people who want part-wolves? Is it a status thing?"

"Don't know," Dick answered. "I don't understand."

I patted Nooky's head. "She's wolfish enough for me."

We didn't resume our turtle hunt, and the creatures didn't reappear for the rest of the summer.

37

CRAYFISH AND BLOODSUCKERS

By the last week in June, I was dealing like a pro with most outdoor activities, but leeches remained problematic, and I was disturbed, one afternoon, to see the severed walleye head I put on the bottom of the minnow trap as bait writhing as if it were alive. Ugh! Myriads of slimy black leeches were feasting on its flesh. Carefully avoiding these disgusting creatures, I gritted my teeth and, with a heave, pulled the wire mesh of the trap out of the water, then held it away from my body as several leeches fell through the grid and landed on the ground at my feet, where they continued to writhe briefly in the hot afternoon sun. I set down the trap a full canoe length away to avoid any contact with the leeches. I hate those things.

I'd placed the fish head in the trap two days ago as bait, hoping to catch a mess of crawfish, and the intrusion of leeches aside, it had done its job. Countless scrabbling crawfish claws grasped the wire mesh, hanging on for dear life. I quickly counted thirty or more little critters. "Aha!" I said aloud, even though Dick was at work and I was alone. "Dinner! I've got enough for dinner!"

Tonight's meal was going to be special, thanks to my catch, and the Time-Life cookbook series.

I loved the recipes in these colorful cookbooks, which often sent me off on new cooking adventures. The *American Food* edition featured a luscious boiled crawfish recipe from Louisiana. I was inspired by the photograph of people gathered around a table, white linen napkins tied around their necks, cracking shells and sucking sweet white meat. And now, with a minnow trap full of these little freshwater crustaceans, I could treat Dick to a crawfish feast, North Woods style.

Unfortunately a roiling mass of leeches still clung to the fish head on the bottom of the trap, and I could see no way to extract the crustaceans without touching some of them. My next task, therefore, was to get rid of the fish head without coming into contact with those loathsome creatures. Eyeballing the crawfish carefully, I decided they were too big to escape through the mesh holes, so my plan was to hold the trap out over the lake, keeping the cover closed, until all the bloodsuckers fell through the mesh into the water. If I had any luck at all, the crawfish would still be clinging to the wires.

With a deep breath, I lifted the minnow trap and held it over the lake. The bloodsuckers stretched themselves, shrank, and wriggled as they dropped through the mesh into the water. The sight was disgusting, and I made certain to keep my hands away from the slimy critters. Finally, the fish head rolled on the bottom of the trap, bloodsucker free. I wanted the leeches away from me.

Now I could safely harvest my crayfish. I ran to the cabin and returned with a bucket and a pair of tongs. I planned to pluck the crayfish out of the trap, plop them in the bucket, and return to the cabin, where I'd bring the water to a boil and add some parsley, onions, and peppercorns. Ta-da: a tasty dinner for my work-worn husband.

But first, I needed to harvest the crayfish. I turned the trap upside down and held it over the bucket, hoping the little shellfish would simply drop in. That didn't happen. The fish head fell out, hit the side of the bucket with a thunk, and dropped to the ground, while the crawfish clung for dear life to the mesh.

Okay, I said to myself, *if that's the way they want to play.* Grasping the biggest crawfish with my tongs, I yanked it loose and transferred it to the bucket, then quickly slapped the cover back on.

As I reached for a second crawfish, a rasping noise caught my ear. I lifted the bucket lid to peek in. The first crawfish was climbing the side, trying to escape. This wouldn't do. I'd worked too hard to lose it now. Slamming the lid shut, I gave the bucket a good thump. There was a small plop as the plucky little creature dropped to the bottom.

Each time I pulled a crawfish from the trap, I was careful to lift the lid on the bucket and drop it in immediately, then slam the bucket shut again. One by one I retrieved the little crustaceans from the minnow trap and transferred them to the bucket.

Although dinner time was approaching, the June sun was still high in the sky when I finally transferred the final crayfish—all in all I'd caught thirty-five—and carried my wild-caught dinner back to the cabin. I was excited.

Lighting a gas burner, I added the seasonings to a pot of water and brought it to a boil. The day was warm, the air steamy with heated water, and I suddenly realized—the time had finally arrived to throw the crawfish in boiling water.

The bucket of crawfish was sitting on the kitchen table, and I could hear scratching noises inside as little claws tried to make their way up the smooth metal sides. I gulped. The doomed crawfish were trying to escape.

A wave of guilt rolled over me. This felt like murder. I was going to throw living, breathing, maybe even feeling creatures into a pot of boiling water. Could I do it?

I thought about releasing them. Should I? Could I? After all this work?

Nah. The cycle of life is brutal, I told myself, and the law of the jungle is eat or get eaten. I'm not a vegetarian, so why be a hypocrite? Someone somewhere was killing the meat I ate. It was time to face up to that reality.

Shaking off any last vestiges of guilt, I wrenched the bucket lid open, held it over the boiling water, and dumped the crawfish in. Once again I heard a faint scratching sound. Could some of the little creatures be trying to climb the smooth sides of the aluminum kettle to escape the boiling water? I cringed. Then I rationalized. This meal will be delicious, and Dick will love it. My feeling of remorse lingered, but the scratching sounds grew more feeble until finally silence filled the cabin, and a rush of relief washed over me.

I let the water simmer for ten minutes, then drained the pot and peered in. The now-cooked crawfish looked like miniscule red lobsters. They also looked delicious. Enough for a meal? I didn't know, but I hoped so after all the fuss.

Taking a good sharp knife, I peeled the shells off the mini-lobsters. Their bodies measured the length of my pointer finger; I was disappointed to find the claws yielded only a toothpick sliver of meat. No matter. I had harvested and killed these creatures and was going to make darn sure not a morsel went to waste.

Half an hour later, tired and disheveled, I carefully set a small bowl of crawfish meat in the coolest spot of the kitchen. One cup. Eight ounces. Not exactly a feast, I thought, opening a can of Hormel chili.

When Dick's canoe pulled up to the dock, I ran down to greet him. "You'll love tonight's appetizers."

The main course for our evening meal was ho-hum canned chili, but the hors d'oeuvres were wonderful. We dipped the tiny white crawfish morsels in butter, and they were as delicious as my Time-Life cookbook claimed.

But I never prepared them again. Too much work for too small a reward. Never again did I want to hear the sound of tiny creatures trying to escape from boiling water. Never.

38

SHOTGUN FOURTH

"How do you use this thing?" I asked as I tried to lift the heavy shotgun to my shoulder. Patiently, Dick once again gave me all the pertinent information regarding the lethal firearm: loading, discharging, the safety catch, aiming, handling the stock. Then we went outside, and I blasted a few practice shots into the air. The noise was enough to break my eardrums, and the recoil bruised my shoulder, but I needed to make sure I knew how to take care of myself during the long hours while Dick was at work. If nothing else, I had to possess enough knowledge to scare off a bear. And the beauty of the shotgun was that I didn't need a good aim. After several loading and trigger-squeezing sessions, Dick felt I knew enough to protect myself if necessary. He set the shotgun alongside the doorway with ammunition close at hand, so I could easily grab, load, and fire it in a hurry.

We had enjoyed a beautiful Fourth of July with my high school friend Mary, and her husband, Ken. Dick was ferrying them back to the Gunflint Trail, and I had my arms elbow deep in soapy water when I heard the distant sound of an outboard motor echoing up the lake. I stopped rattling the dirty silverware in the dishwater, looked up, and listened. Couldn't be Dick yet.

Fishermen frequently came to Tucker on weekends or holidays, so the thrum of a boat motor was no big deal. I ignored it and began drying dishes and stacking them in the cupboard.

But something was different. I stopped. And listened. The growl of the motor grew closer and quit with an abrupt thump. That didn't sound right, and my stomach fluttered as I peeked out the window. The boat wasn't going on past our cabin. No, it had swooped around and was landing at our little log dock.

Three men sat in the boat. I scrutinized them. They looked and acted like nothing more than a bunch of grungy fishermen—harmless enough. *Isn't that what everyone said about the Boston Strangler?* Adopting a "better safe than sorry" approach, I opened the cabin door, stepped hesitantly out, and waved, but stayed on the deck, keeping the shotgun within easy reach.

"Hello," I called. From the vantage point of the deck, I could see that the men were middle-aged, and all three wore well-used fishing vests. If they *were* murderers, then they were murderers who fished.

"Hi," a tall man in a peaked hat called. "We heard about you folks and just wanted to meet the people who spent the winter on Tucker."

I wasn't sure how to respond so I said nothing. After a brief pause, he added, "We saw your husband at the portage, and he told us it was okay to come down here."

"You talked to him?" I asked. That was a relief. If these guys were up to no good, I probably needn't worry. Dick would be back soon and could identify them in a police lineup if necessary. I scrutinized them again and once again failed to see anything unusual or threatening about them. But I stayed cautious. "He won't be gone long," I informed them. "He's taking some friends back to the Trail."

The chilly atmosphere thawed slightly, and they began asking questions.

How was January up here? Cold enough? How do you keep from being bored?

Funny thing was, although we were carrying on a conversation at a near shout, they didn't make any attempt to get out of the boat, and I remained at my perch, safe on the deck.

Finally, after I'd finished explaining the problems of freeze-up and break-up, I felt comfortable enough to invite them on shore. "Why don't you get out and stretch your legs?"

"No, no! That's okay," they chorused.

One of them added, "We just wanted to see your place." Their behavior was beginning to seem downright strange. Staying in the boat, they continued to ask more questions. What about wolves? Did I miss city life? What were our plans for the future?

Finally all the shouting back and forth got ridiculous. "Are you sure you don't want to come on shore?" I asked again, unintentionally sounding a bit irritated.

"Oh no," they all sang again in unison. "We're fine. Just fine." I didn't argue. If they wanted to sit out there in the boat, okay with me.

The fisherman handling the motor finally announced, "We'd better get on with our fishing. We've taken enough of your time." I felt relieved. The entire scene had been goofy. The man in the stern started the motor with a yank, the motor roared to life, and all three of them waved a final, friendly farewell as they continued their cruise down the lake, leaving me peacefully alone again.

They'd barely disappeared around the bend when Dick rounded the bend from the opposite direction.

"Did some fishermen stop by?" he asked as he approached and threw out a line. I grabbed and tied it to the dock.

"Yes. Kind of strange, though. They wouldn't get out of their boat. You saw them on the portage?"

"Yep, I was going out. They were coming in. You say they never got out of the boat?"

I repeated my statement. "No. They sat in it the entire time they were here."

Dick started laughing.

I stared at him. "What's so funny?"

He laughed even harder. "When I met them on the portage, I got a little nervous, seeing they were headed your way, so I told them it was okay to stop and see you, but to be real careful. You were nervous about being alone and had a loaded shotgun right inside the cabin door."

"You didn't really say that, did you?" I asked.

"Yup," he said. "I did. Figured that would keep them on their toes."

"Well, it worked," I said. "If anyone was nervous, those guys were."

39

ALL THAT FREE TIME

People always asked the same question: What do you do with all that free time?

I was thinking about that one beautiful July day as I gazed at the cloudless blue sky. With the July Fourth holiday behind us, the weather was in full summer mode. A light breeze filled the air with the scent of pines. Lake waters lapped gently at the shore. I sat in my beach chair and lifted my face to the hot sun. *This is great*, I said to myself. *A perfect summer day. And I'm getting a fabulous tan.*

It was true, Dick was working long hours. But right now, there was nothing I could do to change our situation. I figured someday his turn to lounge would come. Meanwhile, it would be a crime if I didn't thoroughly enjoy this magnificent summer.

Glancing at my watch I realized I had another hour of leisure before starting dinner. Tonight, I'd prepare the two walleye I'd pulled from the lake earlier, rolling the fillets in potato flour, then frying them in hot oil until they were crispy brown. I'd serve them with homemade sourdough bread that I'd baked that morning, and we'd have apple pie for dessert. Apple pie had been yesterday's baking project.

Money was in short supply and the grocery store was hours away, so I often baked things from scratch. Cakes, pies, bread, and cookies rolled out of my Coleman oven like a production line. The best time for working in front of a hot stove was early morning, before the day's heat started hammering on the cabin roof.

Today had been a good day. I started baking early in the morning, right after Dick began his canoe commute. After baking several loaves of bread and a batch of ginger cookies for Dick's upcoming lunches, I'd flipped a few casts into the lake and caught a walleye. Not enough for our meal, but I put it in a wire cage. I kept the rod and reel handy and cast out Rapalas now and then throughout the day. If I didn't catch enough for a meal, I'd set the first one free.

Midmorning, my major summer painting project filled my time. Striving to make the cabin decor look cozy, I'd already painted a cabinet antique pink and the asbestos sheeting behind the fireplace a cheery gold. I'd even painted the deck the same color. Today, I painted the ash pail antique pink—the only remaining paint I had.

Nooky was my faithful companion during my long days alone. She kept busy with her own projects, chasing red squirrels, watching me cast rod and reel with an avid eye (she loved fish), and burrowing in her hollow under the cabin where she napped in the cool darkness.

After painting the ash pail, I left it to dry on a newspaper page and trotted out to my small garden. I scrutinized the lettuce. Something was eating it! Lettuce grew quite well in my peculiar North Woods soil, but once the woodchucks and insects got through with it, not much ever reached my table. The green beans were coming along nicely, and I thrilled to the sight of my one row of sweet corn. The stalks were springing upward vigorously. On the other hand, the carrot seeds had failed to germinate. Today, I replanted the carrot row, then dug a small hole, and buried last night's potato peels and coffee grounds. It was my method of speed-composting.

Satisfied with today's gardening, I ambled back down to the lake, threw out a few casts, and was thrilled to catch another walleye. That made two fish for dinner.

Now, as I lay in the chaise longue and enjoyed the warm sun, I realized how lucky I was. I was busy, happy, and healthy, and would probably never again in my life experience so relaxed a summer. In a few hours, I would hear the boat motor coming down the lake. The dog would run to greet Dick, and I would saunter inside, fix dinner, and heap our plates with fresh food. Dick and I would eat our evening meal at the little table overlooking the clear waters of Tucker Lake, and if we were lucky, a moose or maybe a beaver might swim across the lake right before our eyes.

40

The Refrigerator Saga

"Water water everywhere, and not a drop to drink."
That wasn't exactly true. We had an entire lake full of drinkable water, but it was warm and getting warmer by the day. Locals bemoaned this as an unusually hot summer, and from the feel of Tucker Lake, I agreed. Our drinking water wasn't cold any longer; heck, it wasn't even cool, and as the summer heat increased, so did its temperature.

Drinking tepid water, lukewarm lemonade, and worst of all, warm beer, was getting to be old hat. I hadn't minded the lack of ice and refrigeration earlier in the summer, but by the third week of July, Dick and I would have killed for a glass of ice-cold water. So when an opportunity popped up, we took it.

According to the Gunflint Trail word-of-mouth news telegraph (a phenomena I never fully understood), someone told Kermit who told Dick that a used gas refrigerator was for sale at Borderland Lodge. "We have to at least take a look at it," I declared.

We took advantage of Dick's next work-free day and gunned the Bronco up the Trail to see if this refrigerator was worth anything. As we pulled up behind the lodge it came into view, standing alongside one of the storage sheds: a bulky, white, old-fashioned refrigerator, in great shape for its age, as if it had just been removed from a movie set. None of that mattered. The important thing was, it worked. We nodded at each other. "We'll take it," Dick said, plunking down the asking price of twenty-five dollars.

"Is it okay if we pick it up next week?" he asked. "We aren't prepared to move it today, and I don't get another day off until then." The owner said yes, looking quite happy at the prospect of getting rid of the old thing.

As we returned to the cabin, I remained giddy at the prospect of refrigeration at my fingertips, but I began seriously wondering how we were going to transport it in a canoe over a portage and two lakes. I usually left such technical and mechanical matters up to Dick, but I did have one idea. "Who can we ask to help us?"

Dick's forehead wrinkled in concentration. "Unfortunately for us, I can't think of any old friends or relatives visiting during my long weekend, and we can't ask a mere acquaintance."

I gulped. We'd have to do this thing ourselves.

"Don't worry. We can do it," Dick said.

I wondered how.

That evening we relaxed on the deck. The sun was setting, and the lake looked like a mirror, but we hardly noticed it. We were deep in discussion. "We've got the outrigger, and that will really make a difference." Dick was referring to a fiberglass outrigger he'd made to steady the effects of a side-mounted motor on our double-ended canoe.

"Uh huh," was my doubtful answer.

"We'll take our time, go nice and slow, and everything will be fine. I'll build a skid to cross the portage," Dick promised. "We'll use our brains. We won't tie down the refrigerator, so if it does go overboard, we won't go with it. But don't worry. That won't happen. We'll just be real careful."

"Uh huh," was my grim reply.

He continued. "I'll build a shelter behind the cabin, and we'll keep it there."

I nodded. *If we ever get that far.*

⁓

The fateful day (forever to be remembered as Refrigerator Moving Day) began with overcast skies that threatened rain. No matter. We had no choice. Dick had the day off from work. We'd promised to move the refrigerator today. No backing out.

Like warriors preparing for battle, we uttered phrases of fake bravado. "Think of how good a cold beer will taste. Think of eating fresh meat anytime, and vegetables. Think of refrigerator shelves filled with beef steaks, strawberries, milk, Dr. Pepper, and Hamm's Beer." We readied ourselves for the big day, dressing in comfortable garb—old jeans, ratty t-shirts, rubber boots.

We also filled a backpack with work gloves, rain gear, water, and several sandwiches. What to do with Nooky perplexed us. She'd take up space in the canoe, but we didn't feel right about leaving her alone since we had no idea how long this venture would take.

Finally we decided to bring her. When we called, she came running from behind the cabin, where she'd been chasing Bonnie and Clyde, our resident gray jays. As she hopped in the canoe, tail wagging, I told her, "You have no idea what you're getting into."

Crossing both lakes and driving up the Gunflint, I tried not to think of the hardship ahead. *Take one thing at a time.* I gritted my teeth. *Relax and take a deep breath. One thing at a time.* I repeated this mantra every time a negative thought rushed over me.

Too soon, our trip ended. I swallowed hard and watched Nooky peer out the windows of our Bronco as we pulled into the resort and slowly drove up to the storage building.

"There is it," Dick said as he stopped the vehicle and jumped out. A hulking white Servel refrigerator sat up against the structure where we'd first glimpsed it. "Recognize it?"

I gulped. It hadn't been that humongous two weeks ago, had it? I felt gobsmacked. It must have grown, put on weight. For the life of me, I couldn't remember the refrigerator being as huge as it now appeared. But then, I hadn't planned for the two of us to carry it ourselves.

Getting out of the car, I took a few steps and stopped. Had I really agreed to this folly? My stomach dropped, but I managed to move forward.

I glanced at Dick, who was walking around the beast, showing no signs of nerves. I supposed he was figuring his next move. I had no such thoughts. I was wondering if we could get our twenty-five dollars back.

At that moment, one of the resort's employees saw us and took pity. He ran over and helped Dick hoist the refrigerator into the back of the Bronco.

My shoulders sank as the inevitable settled in. No turning back now. We were in for it.

I opened the car door, slumped down in the front seat, and waited. Thoughts swirled through my head. I should never had agreed to this nonsense. I wished I could feel as positive as Dick, but I was just plain worried.

Fifteen minutes passed while Dick tied the hulking white object down and I chewed my cuticles.

Finally we turned around slowly and headed down the driveway away from the resort and onto the gravel road leading to the Gunflint Trail.

At this point, Dick sped up slightly. I managed to swallow my fears and watched to make sure the car motion didn't loosen the cords tying down the refrigerator. We drove to the old game warden shack on Little Iron, where Dick backed the car as close as possible to the lake.

Grimly, I assessed the situation. The next task was to get this enormous appliance onto the canoe gunnels. My watch read 1:20 P.M., which sent a shock down my spine. Already? Time was moving too fast. A few drops of rain spattered out of the sodden gray skies. My heart sank. Rain would really complicate things.

But Dick was unfazed. "Okay, let's move it," he said, hopping out of the car. "Got your gloves on?"

Following him, I squared my shoulders, gritted my teeth, and grabbed the refrigerator. It was hard to get a grip, but I managed. Pushing and straining, we slowly eased the hulk from the open tailgate onto the 2 x 4s that Dick had fastened onto the boat's gunnels. We moved at a snail's pace and stopped often to deliberate but finally wriggled the beast in place.

I couldn't help sighing with relief when we finally got the refrigerator balanced, like a beached whale, across the width of the boat. It had seemed an impossible situation, but we did it. It was too early to feel victory, but as I waited for Dick to park our vehicle, I felt my first slight surge of optimism. We might just pull this off!

Dick returned, carefully stepped in, and took his place by the motor.

Moving with painfully slow motions, I guided Nooky into the craft. Carefully pushing the boat into the water, I ever so gently slid onto my seat. Dick started the motor, and our entourage began to move over the waters of Little Iron towards the portage. Dick was right. The outrigger helped stabilize the canoe and keep it upright.

The raindrops were getting larger, falling with big plopping splashes, but mercifully the wind was negligible. I pictured how we would look from above, how we must look to an eagle. Two people, a dog, and a large white box floating down the lake in a narrow aluminum vessel.

Dick had the throttle down as far as it would go, so the

boat was barely moving. I hardly dared breathe for fear of tipping. And I was beginning to wonder, for the first time, how we would ever get this thing across the portage. Dick had said we'd pull it, but I hadn't paid much attention to his explanations. Perhaps I didn't imagine we'd get that far.

I soon found out. Dick turned off the motor and with careful motions guided us into the small bay of the portage. Rain was falling, but the lake waters stayed still and flat. Gingerly, he stepped out while I held Nooky in check.

In a few minutes the real work would begin—unloading the refrigerator and hauling it across the muddy, rock-strewn, three-hundred-foot portage. I tried to prepare mentally. While Dick held the watercraft steady, I inched the dog and myself very carefully onto shore. Already I felt exhausted, and my hands and back ached. I wanted to collapse on a log and rest, but instead I watched as Dick directed our next move.

He'd built a skid—a sledlike apparatus with tapered runners at the prow and a rope tied to the front—and left it in the woods nearby. I was impressed. But there was no time for rest. I watched as he dragged it out from its hiding place and moved it near the water's edge and our partially beached boat.

We took our positions on either side of the canoe. "Lift on the count of three," he commanded. My gloved hands gripped the rear of the refrigerator. Dick grabbed the front.

"One, two, three!" We lifted in unison and carefully inched the refrigerator off the gunnels and, pushing and pulling, we proceeded by infinitesimal degrees to slide it onto the skid. Every inch of movement was a huge effort. When it was finally in place, we sat together on a mossy rock to rest.

But not for long. More heavy work lay in store. When air had returned to my lungs and I was breathing normally again, I walked to the front of the skid and placed the rope around my waist. Dick positioned himself at the back, holding a pry bar. On the count of three, I pulled and Dick pushed. Inch by inch, foot by foot, we moved the refrigerator over the rocky, uneven ground of the portage.

Crunch. I stopped. We weren't moving. I looked. The skid runner was hung up on a rock.

"What is it?" Dick ran forward.

"Just a rock," I said in a faint voice.

We both pulled, and with a lot of grinding and groaning we finally moved the skid off the rock. Dick trudged back to the rear, and we began our tedious forward motion again.

The next two hours were filled with my pulling, Dick's pushing, and an occasional double forward action from both of us when a rock caught a runner. We and the refrigerator were the only objects moving in the softly falling rain. Everything else was motionless. Even the dog stood stock still for long periods as she watched our strange behavior.

Stopping momentarily, I wiped sweat from my grimy forehead and adjusted the red bandana covering my hair. I had no idea what thoughts were passing through Dick's mind, but I had some pretty interesting ones. Homicide, for example. That is, of my husband. Divorce was another, but neither seemed to solve the immediate problem, and I knew once this journey was over, I'd probably stay married.

After two hours of marathon physical labor, I glimpsed the thinning trees ahead that signaled the end of the portage. Then, without fanfare, we were suddenly there! All the backbreaking work had paid off. I could have cried for joy. Mud-spattered and bedraggled, we stopped briefly to catch our breaths and take a short rest.

But within minutes, we were on the move again. Dick portaged the canoe, and we began the task of loading up the refrigerator for the last leg of the trip. Though the process was painstakingly slow, it almost seemed easy after the long, painful portage crossing.

Once Dick had started the motor and we were on our way, a

strange thing happened. I'd been nervous all day, but now, suddenly, horrible images filled my imagination. What if the canoe tipped over after all our work and the refrigerator plummeted to the lake bottom? The thought was unbearable, and I hunkered down on the seat, not moving a muscle, filled with a sense of foreboding, almost of panic.

Nooky sensed my tenseness, and she too sat still as a mouse, watching with anxious eyes. We wore life jackets and the dog could swim, so I didn't fear for our lives, but the thought of losing our prized refrigerator after all this work—that was intolerable!

The final three-mile jaunt was painstakingly slow. I gripped the sides of the canoe, chewing my upper lip, and watched the rust-colored water of Tucker Lake slide under the overburdened canoe. We passed through the narrows, the comforting sight of its rock cliffs speaking of home. When I saw the fallen pine tree on the point, I knew we were almost there. The cabin lay just around the corner. I should have felt relief when Dick carefully pulled the canoe up to the dock. Our ordeal was almost over, but I was as worried as ever that during our final task of skidding the refrigerator from canoe to shore, we might drop the hulking kitchen appliance in the water and be left with only a useless pile of metal to remind us of this day.

Dick might have had the same thought. I noticed worry flicker across his face as I carefully stepped from the canoe.

"Last time!" Dick's voice was edged with fatigue.

"Let's do it!" I sounded much braver than I felt. We slowly skidded the refrigerator from the 2 x 4s on the canoe's gunnels to shore. Dick's face was lined with exhaustion as we pulled and pushed. My shaking arms couldn't last much longer. We threw our last ounces of energy into a few final tugs and suddenly— the nightmare was over. The refrigerator lay on its side, safe on the beach. Safe on solid land.

"That's it for today," Dick said. Raindrops still fell gently from the sky. "We'll haul it behind the cabin tomorrow."

Proudly I looked at our prize. The big white Servel rested, also looking exhausted. We were now owners of a refrigerator and all the wonderful food and drink it would hold.

The next day, we moved it into a shed behind the cabin, let it sit for twenty-four hours to release Freon bubbles, and went to town where we bought a propane tank, beef steaks, and a Hamm's tapper.

When we got home, we placed the little aluminum keg in the soon-to-be cold air of our new refrigerator. I've never tasted any liquid as good as that first glass of cold beer.

We still have the tapper.

41

Blueberry Time

Suddenly August arrived. With it came cooler temperatures, fewer bugs, a slight nip in the morning air...and a flood of visitors. Email, texting, and cell phones were still a thing of the future, but we managed to communicate with everyone. Family and friends who were hoping to visit wrote letters or left messages with Loon Lake Lodge to set up meeting times, and if someone was an hour or so late, the other party waited. No problem.

Dick's parents visited first. We all arrived promptly at our meeting spot, and Dick and I carried their baggage to the canoe. They climbed in, and we set off for the cabin. Dick's mother, Katherine, was a berry picker, and as he guided the canoe down Tucker, she and I discussed picking prospects.

"I saw what looked like a good blueberry patch on the other side of the narrows," Dick interrupted. "I'll take you there tomorrow."

"Great," Katherine said.

"I've only seen a few plants around the cabin," I said. "Maybe we'll have better luck tomorrow."

Dick kicked in the throttle, and we surged home to enjoy a meal of polish sausages and beer provided by his parents.

The air was cool the next morning as Katherine and I settled into the canoe. I wore a bandana over my pigtails and carried an empty lard bucket for berries. I'd given Katherine an empty peanut butter bucket.

"Aren't you wearing shoes?" Katherine called over the motor's roar as we sped down the lake. She pointed to my bare feet.

"No. I usually don't wear shoes in summer."

"Don't your feet hurt?" She looked perplexed.

"Nope." I lifted a calloused foot in the air. "They toughened up early in spring."

Maybe I am kind of a hippie, I thought, watching her smile. I'd been going barefoot my entire life. Each spring, I delighted in ditching my uncomfortable shoes to spend the summer running free.

Dick pulled the canoe up to the berry patch he'd spotted, and Katherine and I clambered out. "Looks good," Katherine said, pointing to a small field where blueberry bushes grew. But it turned out there were few actual berries on the bushes. We tramped over rocks and underbrush, tree roots and grass, but managed to scrounge up only a scant pint.

"We have enough for muffins," Katherine announced cheerfully an hour later as we climbed back into the canoe, carrying our treasures. When we arrived back at the cabin I fired up my Coleman oven, Katherine cleaned the berries, I stirred up a batch of dough, and we baked blueberry muffins.

Dick took his father fishing that afternoon. The day had warmed—not good for fishing—but despite the hot August sun, they caught two nice walleyes. I fried them for dinner. For dessert, we gobbled down the fresh blueberry muffins.

I felt a vague sense of relief the next morning as I waved good-bye to Dick's parents, followed by a twinge of guilt. But more company was on the way, and I had a lot of preparation ahead. Once Dick had ferried his parents to their car, he hurried back to help ready the cabin for the next set of guests—my parents. Their visit would be followed by a former co-worker of Dick's and his two children. Finally, my brother and his friend, Pete, planned to camp on the island across the lake.

We'd never been so popular in our lives.

42

DEBUT OF A WOODSWOMAN

We'd developed an efficient protocol for entertaining guests, and it was a good thing since the next few weeks were filled with visitors. We showed them the open-air toilet, fed them walleye, and encouraged everyone to bring at least one meal to share. I was surprised and relieved that our role as wilderness hosts hadn't made much of a dent in our dwindling bank account.

I enjoyed seeing people from the Cities. My parents' visit was short. They spent their nights at Loon Lake Lodge, opting not to sleep on our hard bunk bed, and Dick ferried them to and fro. Dick's work friend brought his children, but his ten-year-old daughter's homesickness sent them home earlier than planned. My brother and his friend camped on the little island across the lake and joined us for meals, and also spent a lot of time fishing and canoeing.

Finally the spate of company subsided, and we were alone. Our solitude was cut short, however, when a local couple asked us to dinner. We had met them last winter at Loon Lake Lodge, and Dick saw them occasionally when they stopped to chat as he checked the mailbox.

"That's great," I said when he told me that evening about the prospective visit as we ate a tuna casserole. Getting to know more locals appealed to me.

"Only problem is," Dick swallowed a forkful, "transportation. They live ten miles from Grand Marais, and if you come with me in the morning and spend the day in town, you'll have to drive all the way back up the Trail to pick me up after work and then we'll be forced to drive almost all the way back to Grand Marais to their house. Not to mention, you were just in town yesterday."

I had an idea. I wasn't sure it was a good one, and my voice betrayed my uncertainty. "I could walk out to the Trail…go through the woods and meet you. But I don't know…it's kind of scary, being alone and all."

His face brightened. He wasn't the least bit uncertain. "You can do it. Follow the path we marked when the lake ice was breaking up. Bring a compass. Go slow. The trail is clearly marked. You'll be fine."

I was flattered. He clearly believed in my navigational skills, but I wasn't so sure.

"I guess I could," I said.

The day came, and as I prepped for the walk, I tied my shoe-laces, adjusted the blue bandana covering my hair, and asked myself, *Am I really ready for this?* Was I actually going to walk from our cabin to the Gunflint Trail alone, through the woods, by myself?

Yes. I can do this. I can do this, I thought. I'll use my common sense and will not get lost. After re-checking my backpack, which held a compass, a water bottle, and a can of bug dope (very, very necessary), I shouldered it and headed out the door. Time to quit stalling and get moving.

Nooky pulled at her leash, unhappy with captivity, but I counted on her to help find the trail should I lose my way, and I couldn't risk having her run off. Taking a deep breath, I walked resolutely into the woods. Nooky pulled again at her leash. "You have to stay hooked up," I told her. "I don't want you running after deer."

The afternoon sun was bright, but a slight breeze and the forest shade made walking comfortable. Surprisingly, the trail was easy to follow, though we hadn't walked it recently. The first stretch was simple, and I strode confidently, soon finding myself at the spruce swamp. Here I lost some of my self-assurance. The path veered east. Would I find it?

I turned and examined the tall black trunks carefully, looking for the correct marker. My eyes moved slowly to the southeast. Nothing. I moved them in the opposite direction.

Yes. Finally, there it was—the giant tentacles of the uprooted spruce tree that marked the way. The partridge that always flew from somewhere in its dark recesses was silent today or maybe gone. I swerved to the right. Nooky looked at me approvingly. "I may not have a good nose like you do," I said, "but we humans can find our way too." It was comforting to talk to someone, even a dog.

The next segment turned and twisted but was easy to follow. I felt quite relaxed walking along the ridge running parallel to the Tucker River. And then, through the trees, I spotted the green water of the river flowing below. My next move would be to follow the path along the river's ridge through the dappled birch tree shadows, then head downhill to the log "bridge" where Nooky had gone under last April. Today, the river was low, a mere trickle.

I started down the path, happy that so far, the walk had been easy.

Crack!

My heart stopped. What was that? I swung sharply around.

Another crack!

Nooky strained on her leash and growled. Something was nearby. I pulled her closer and looped my trembling fingers around her collar buckle, ready to release it if a bear crashed out of the woods. We stayed this way for several petrifying moments. Then, a blur of white tail and the reddish coat of a deer flashed and disappeared into the green underbrush. I gave a huge sigh of relief. Nooky, however, looked irritated. She'd been ready for a good chase.

"Back to work," I told her, and we bounded the rest of the way down the hill and stepped lightly over the little log bridge across the river. We trudged up the steep hill on the opposite shore and headed directly north through another spruce swamp. Usually, the mossy green hummocks and eerie black tree trunks fascinated me, but today was different. No time to enjoy the scenery.

Although the deer had startled me, nervousness hadn't taken over. I tried to stay alert and concentrate on my surroundings. So far, this tactic was working. My next challenge was finding the island of birch that signaled another turn.

There it was. My shoulders loosened with relief as I spotted the white trunks. Reaching it, I turned west and kept a straight line through a small alder brush swamp, letting the dog lead with her nose to the ground. She seemed to sense the end was near, and moving faster and faster, within minutes she guided me to the tracks of an old overgrown logging road. Jubilantly, I turned north. "We did it, Nooky! We did it!" She jumped and gave my face a lick. I had the unflattering feeling she was more relieved than I was, which doesn't say much for her trust in my navigational skills.

The rest was a piece of cake. The final leg followed an old weed-choked road—not much of a road, but it ran smack-dab into the Gunflint Trail. Soon I heard the high pitched whine of car engines. A big grin broke out on my face as I realized I'd gotten through the woods alone! I glanced at my watch. It had taken only an hour, which meant I was early. Dick wouldn't be leaving work for another thirty minutes.

Feeling sassy and proud, I strolled up to the asphalt of the Gunflint Trail, touched it with my toe—just to say I did it—and sat down in a grassy spot on the upper side of the ditch to wait for Dick, wondering what I looked like to the people in passing cars. A resting hitchhiker? A long-distance trekker? I didn't care; I was enjoying the moment. A blue jay squawked. Nooky curled up in the grass beside me. I was bursting with pride. I felt I could now call myself a bona fide woodswoman.

43

A Capful of Mushrooms

"Look at those mushrooms! They're huge!" Al's excited voice echoed as he dropped to his knees and peered into the yellowing underbrush.

What did he mean? I didn't see any mushrooms. I looked closer, and there they were, small and white, sprouting under logs and popping out from under fallen leaves. We were crossing the portage on a sunny day in late August with Al, the eccentric bachelor from Gunflint Lake, on our way to the cabin.

Al continued. "I've never seen so many of these mushrooms —and so big! We've got to pick them," he urged. "This is really special. I really have never seen so many good ones."

Dick and I stared at him. He wasn't actually talking about picking mushrooms, was he?

Our skepticism must have showed because Al continued. "Don't worry. It'll be okay. I know only this one species. They're safe to eat, and I'm very familiar with them. They'll be delicious." His voice took on a commanding edge. "C'mon. Start picking."

Normally Al was a passive man, and I'd never heard him bark out orders, so I dropped to the forest floor and started picking the rather ordinary looking fungi. The ferns and thimbleberry leaves were starting to wither and turn yellow, making it easy to find and pick the mushrooms.

I twisted my blue bandana handkerchief into a little pouch and filled it. Dick filled his hat, and Al took off his ancient, never-seen-the-inside-of-a-washing-machine cap and used it as a mushroom container. When all our hats were full, we filled jacket pockets and kept picking until we could think of nowhere else to put them. Finally, we climbed into the canoe and went home.

Al raved about our good luck all the way home. Mushrooms were one of his favorite dishes... he'd show me how to cook them... they'd be delicious... and did we know just how lucky we were to have stumbled upon this treasure?

I was ambivalent. How different could they be from store-bought mushrooms?

When we reached the cabin, Al gave Dick a quick tutorial on the dos and don'ts of mushroom appearances. They should be white with no pink gills. Other than that, they should "look like the ones you see at the store except maybe a little smaller. Ask me if you aren't sure." I'd thrown all the mushrooms in a large plastic bowl, and with their heads bent the two men sat in the late afternoon shade on the deck and culled through the fungi.

Occasionally I heard Dick asking Al to check one he wasn't sure about. When they finally finished, they brought the mushroom-filled bowl to me.

Following Al's instructions, I hauled out the cast-iron frying pan and browned chopped onions in bacon fat (in those days, all good cooks kept a bacon fat supply), then gently sautéed the mushrooms with the onions.

When the mushrooms had reached an appropriate level of tenderness—Al supervised this stage by tasting one—I lifted the pan from the heat at exactly the right moment, and we sat down to feast. Mushrooms were the whole meal, and what a meal. They were rich and flavorful; I've never tasted mushrooms as delicious since. Al was right. We had stumbled onto a treasure.

Dusk was beginning to fall, so Al buttoned his plaid flannel shirt and picked up the hatchet he always carried when in the woods, prepping for his usual trek through the forest to the Gunflint Trail. Before disappearing into the underbrush, he said in a jocular tone. "If you see buzzards circling over the woods tomorrow, come looking for my body. Ha,ha,ha."

I was startled and suddenly recalled stories of people who picked and ate the wrong mushrooms and died horrible deaths. What if even *one* mushroom had been poisonous?

I glanced at Dick. He avoided my eyes.

"I'm just kidding," Al added. "The mushrooms were perfectly safe."

"Ha ha." We joined his laughter and waved good-bye.

"He was joking, wasn't he?" I asked, starting to feel anxious, as Al disappeared into the moose maples behind the cabin.

A strange look crossed Dick's face.

"What?" My heart sank. I demanded. "What do you know?"

Dick was hesitant. "You know when Al and I were cleaning mushrooms out on the deck?"

"Yes…"

"Well, he occasionally tossed out a questionable mushroom, and he was pretty relaxed about supervising me."

"Oh no." I said. My stomach knotted. "Is that all?"

"Umm. No." Again Dick hesitated. "I showed him one that looked suspicious and asked, how about this one? It's got pinkish gills." 'Oh throw that one out,' said Al casually, without missing a beat."

Dick looked at me. "I started wondering. Did we cull all the poisonous ones? Al was pretty lackadaisical."

My stomach lurched at the word *poisonous*. It gave an ominous gurgle. "Did you say anything?" I wondered.

"No." Dick said in a tone that surprised me with its calmness. "Sometimes you have to have faith."

"Faith!" I squawked. "Faith?

"Too late now." Dick answered. "Besides, Al is an expert."

"So he says." The rumbles in my stomach grew louder. Dire what-ifs circled in my head. What if I'd accidentally eaten a poisonous mushroom? What if Al's judgment was wrong? He was a World War II veteran. What if he wasn't frightened of death?

Feeling worse by the minute, I glanced at Dick. He was slightly green around the gills.

"Does your stomach feel funny?" I asked.

"Yeah." He looked uncomfortable. "Probably my imagination."

"We'd better hope," I said, trying to ignore my burbling intestines.

The next few hours passed in slow motion. Part of me wondered if I was dying, while the other part figured I was fine and chalked up my upset stomach to nothing more than a vivid imagination. I washed dishes with a bubbling stomach. Dick sat on the deck and tried to relax his gurgling innards. I joined him, and we watched the evening descend with rumbling guts.

"I'm sure the mushrooms were just fine," I said, trying to assure both Dick and myself. "Al is such a cautious person."

"I hope so," Dick said. We looked at each other. Was he really?

"How's your stomach?" I asked.

"Still iffy."

"Mine too." We were quiet, the only sounds our growling stomachs.

We sat for a long time watching the sun set. Finally, we could no longer see the pine tree on the island across the lake. During that time my stomach burbling had turned into a murmuring, then the murmuring subsided into occasional whines, and finally a random ping. Feeling hopeful, I glanced at Dick. "Do you feel better?"

"Yeah. Just now. Maybe we're going to live."

We laughed, but our yucks sounded hollow. "Did we really think Al would endanger our lives?"

"Nah." Dick said. "But my gut sure did."

I yawned. "I feel absolutely exhausted. Think I'll get ready for bed."

"Me too." Dick stood up. "At least we won't have to sleep on upset stomachs."

My bedtime preps were almost enjoyable, I was so happy the war in my stomach had ended.

We stepped outside with toothbrushes and water mugs and brushed our teeth as we always did, spitting into the underbrush. "Now that I know we aren't going to die," Dick swished his toothbrush in his mug then emptied it in the underbrush. "I figure we ate too much too fast. We pigged out."

"Silly us. It was indigestion all the time. I'll tell you though, those mushrooms were the best I've ever eaten."

"They were," Dick agreed.

"I don't think I'd do it over again, though," I said.

The next morning we checked the sky for buzzards just in case. Who knows? Al could have tripped and fallen on his ax. We saw nothing but blue sky and white clouds.

44

DOING IT OUR WAY

I gunned our Bronco as I sped up the Trail, venting my frustration. September had arrived and the moose maple along the roadside flamed red, but I was blind to the beauty. While running errands and grocery shopping in Grand Marais, I'd talked to an acquaintance who gave me some depressing and infuriating news.

Earlier in August I'd sent my resume and job application form to the local school district, feeling optimistic, and I was surprised when I didn't even receive the courtesy of a reply.

Now I knew why. The superintendent hadn't even looked at my credentials. He assumed Dick and I were hippies, and he didn't mind telling people about it. Any available teaching job for me was out of the question. I couldn't believe it. How dare he? He didn't know me. Furious, as I drove I mumbled imaginary conversations with a man I'd never met, telling him exactly what I thought of him in no uncertain terms.

Meanwhile, Dick's job on the drilling rig was scheduled to end the first week of October, and he needed to find more work. I wanted to help with our new lives by bringing home a second check. It was *so* frustrating.

Relaxing on the deck on a long summer weekend was one of our favorite activities. Nooky's beloved burrow is under our feet and farther back.

When I finally reached Loon Lake Lodge and delivered the twenty pounds of potatoes the Johnsons had ordered from town, I shared my woes with Kermit, who looked sheepish.

"Have you heard that too?" I asked. "That we're hippies?" An uncomfortable expression crossed his face.

"Well—," he hemmed and hawed. "Someone did ask me what kind of clothes you guys wore, and I told them you dress like everyone who lives up the Trail."

I knew what prompted that question. People did think we were hippies, meaning they thought Dick had long hair, and I wore granny dresses, and we both sported long strings of love beads around our necks. This made me even angrier. People shouldn't assume anything about us merely because we were living in the wilderness. We were as middle class as they come.

Kermit was sympathetic. He rubbed his hands across his kind but wrinkled face and said, "They don't know you guys. People need to get to know you, and they'll like you. It's not easy, moving into a new area and especially a small town. When I moved up here from Duluth years ago, it was hard. Everyone wondered who I was. It's the same with you and Dick. Give it time."

"I suppose," I mumbled. I wasn't convinced, but Kermit was a nice guy, so I smiled, thanked him for the encouragement, and waited till I pulled out of his driveway before pounding on the steering wheel in exasperation. I was still upset.

Later that evening, while watching a golden sunset from the deck, Dick finally grew tired of my complaints.

"We need a pep talk," He said, pulling up his jacket collar. September evenings were cool.

"I guess." I moped. "It just seems so darn unfair. We both have good resumes and experience, but we can't find decent jobs." I stopped and added, "Except that job my former principal at Robbinsdale offered me."

"Yes." Dick honed in. "And what did you do?"

"Turned it down," I admitted.

"And why?"

"Because I don't want to live in the suburbs."

"Let's face it, dear," he said. "I—you—we—have made a choice."

"And there are consequences," I replied, acknowledging the truth I'd been denying all afternoon. I took a sip of my coffee. It had grown cold.

"We had the chance to go back to Minneapolis, buy a house in the suburbs, have a family, move into a bigger house, eventually retire and all that..." Dick pointed out.

"But that's not what we want." I looked across the lake at the birds roosting in the tall pine on the island. "Truth is, I want to live up here, but I really want to help with finances. I want to get settled in. "

"Don't worry so much about finances. Not right now," Dick said. "Men's salaries are better than women's, so I need a job first, something that will get us through the winter. Then next summer maybe we can open a little gift shop and sell glass items that I'll make. I've been thinking about that. All kinds of things are possible. And if the job I get is located here on the Gunflint, we could save money by living in the cabin another winter."

It was true. We did have options. I brightened. A cute little gift shop—that would be fun. People always loved the glass animals and baubles Dick made.

"You're right," I said. "We just have to hold on. At least there's always work in the woods for you." I sighed. "We really did jump off a cliff without knowing what's at the bottom."

"Yes, we did, but don't forget, we knew at the time that we were entering unknown territory. I, for one, don't regret it." He glanced at me, trying to read my expression. "We'll figure things out, but we'll do it our way."

For the first time that day, a sense of well-being filled me, my doubts disappeared, and my spirits lifted. Dick was right. We would find a way.

45

MOOSE GARDENING

Our lives settled into a quiet autumn routine. The days grew shorter. Dick continued to leave for work before the sun rose, while I took care of the cabin. I stopped agonizing over the future. We'd deal with whatever came our way.

One cool, semi-cloudy September morning, I busied myself refreshing sourdough starter. I stepped outside and walked to the small shed where we'd placed the refrigerator. A loud raven squawk sounded somewhere in the forest, but that wasn't unusual, and I paid no attention. Placing the jar of bubbling starter yeast in the refrigerator, I returned to the cabin and had barely closed the door when a crash sounded outside. *What could that be?* I stopped and listened. Nooky's ears cocked. Another loud crack sounded. Something was in the woods behind the cabin.

Cautiously, I turned my head far enough to see through the rear cabin window and abruptly stopped. Something brown was out there. A frisson of fear swept over me, but at the same time I was curious and inched closer for a look. When I finally recognized the brown form, I gasped. A large cow moose, with huge hooves planted smack dab in the middle of my garden, stared back at me. She wasn't ten feet away on the other side of the wall.

Her long, homely face looked startled.

She stood motionless, brown shoulders hunched. Her eyes moved as she swung an incongruously small head slowly from side to side. Her little ears twitched. I stared at her. She stared at me.

During the stare-down, a flood of questions ran through my mind. What was she thinking? Was she wondering why a human was in her domain? I was mesmerized. I'd never been this close to a living, breathing moose before.

Meanwhile, my two surviving tomato plants were turning into sauce under the creature's heavy weight. Nooky was infuriated and barked the high-pitched yowl she reserved for such "big game" occasions, but she was inside, and the moose totally ignored her.

Lady moose shifted her legs slightly. *No! Don't knock down my only surviving cornstalk*, I pleaded. *And please don't trample that small bush of green beans.* A few ears of corn and the green beans were all that was left of my once-high gardening hopes.

If she didn't get out of my garden soon, her restless hooves would uproot all my veggies—stalks, leaves, and all—churning them into the ground. I needed to act. Our deep interspecies communication had gone on long enough. She needed to get the heck out of my poor garden. I hadn't busted my butt all summer for her to ruin it.

I cleared my throat, opened the little kitchen window, took a deep breath, and yelled at the top of my lungs. "Get out of my garden!"

The sound of my shrill voice sent Nooky into a frenzy. She yipped and whined. The cow moose turned her head to better see the source of the noise. "Scat!" I shouted, wondering how I could possible yell any louder. "Move!"

Not a moose eyelid stirred. Not a haunch muscle quivered. Not a hoof wiggled. Flabbergasted, I stared. She wasn't moving. I looked at her long legs and gigantic body, wondering how much she weighed. A thousand pounds? Who knew? A lot.

A minute passed, and still she refused to move. I shouted again. "Go! Get out of here!" Nothing. Not even an ear twitch. Nooky howled, crazy at being trapped inside, unable to chase this creature. She stopped briefly at my feet and stared beseechingly at me.

"No. I'm not letting you out!" She lifted her muzzle and yowled again.

The moose and I were at an impasse. The beast seemed unperturbed. Was she deaf? Was she hiding from an overzealous bull moose? It was rutting season. Who could say?

How could I get rid of this creature before she totally decimated the last vestiges of my garden produce? I renewed my yelling efforts. "Scat. Shoo. Get. GO!" Nooky continued to bark. Lady moose ignored the ruckus.

Finally, when I began to despair, something spurred her to action. I had no idea what, but my jaw dropped as, slowly and with dignity, she turned her huge head to face the woods and, taking her sweet time, stepped out of the garden and ambled away through the underbrush at a leisurely pace. Though I had no idea what finally prompted her to depart, I heaved a sigh of relief and sat down, exhausted by all the noise and emotional turmoil. Nooky kept whining, her ears staying flat, disappointed at not being allowed to give chase.

I waited until the moose's crashing sounds no longer echoed through the woods, then I high-tailed it out to the garden to assess the damage. Nooky followed, sniffing hoof tracks, growling, and throwing menacing glances into the woods.

"She won't come back," I told her, but she cocked her head, still hopeful. I turned my attention back to what remained of my garden.

Her hooves had trampled not only the tomatoes, but also the comfrey plant Al had given me. Rats! I'd forgotten about that. I felt like crying.

All summer I'd been fighting for my garden. Unsuccessfully. My first lettuce planting had been decimated by insects. The second lettuce planting and a thriving carrot crop fell victim to a woodchuck even though I'd set Nooky on it several nights in a row. Somehow the chubby brown creature always managed to get away.

If not for all the intrusions, I'm sure my garden would have been a success. Thanks to the influence of Ruth Stout's book *How to Have a Green Thumb without an Aching Back,* I'd faithfully plowed coffee grounds, eggshells, and other organic matter into the soil all summer, and it was rich and loamy. It would be a great garden next year—with a fence around it.

Now, I scrutinized my remaining harvest—an ear or two of corn that needed ripening and a scattering of green beans. I decided to pick the beans immediately and fix them for dinner. Why risk losing them to another critter? I spent the rest of the day preparing a potato and green bean soup that my mother used to make.

Late afternoon, when Dick came through the door, I was excited to tell him my moose adventure. "You'll never guess what happened—." I started, but before I could launch into my narrative he blurted out excitedly, "There might be a job for me at Arrowhead Electric."

As he sat down to take off his heavy boots, I continued: "That's great. But you'll never guess—."

His excited voice interrupted me again. "I'd like you to go to town tomorrow and call the manager for a job interview. Will you?"

I swallowed my excitement, realizing he was in a different zone than I, and answered. "Sure. I'll go. That's great news."

I waited till we'd eaten most of our supper before I finally said, "You should have seen the big cow moose in my garden today."

46

Dick Loses His Backpack

I had great hopes after setting up a job interview appointment for Dick with Arrowhead Electric Company. A few days later, we drove to the power company in Lutsen and Dick interviewed for the job—and got it. I was elated. Now we could get on with our lives! I could even start looking for a place to rent for the winter. As we headed back up the shore on Highway 61 towards Grand Marais, Dick was smiling, and I didn't blame him.

"I start in three weeks," he said. "The manager wasn't certain of the exact day. They'll let me know, leave a message with Loon Lake."

We celebrated at the A&W in Grand Marais and went home. When we reached the cabin, we unloaded groceries from the canoe and settled in. Dick sat back and relaxed while I fixed a pot of coffee.

Having a job lined up took away a lot of the stress we'd both been feeling. Dick's face looked more relaxed than I'd seen in a while, and I felt a sense of relief too.

"It's been a year since the day we moved here," I said as I poured him a cup of coffee, engulfed by a sudden wave of nostalgia.

Dick nodded. "Remember how worried you were when you and Nooky were waiting on Little Iron and I didn't show up?"

"Yes, and now, I've spent a whole summer alone and don't even worry during the thunderstorms." I poured myself a cup and sat down.

We were silent, sipping our coffee. I was thinking about how fast the year had gone and how I had no regrets about either our decision to move here for the winter or our more radical choice to stay in the area. Dick was deep in his own thoughts. We exchanged a few words about the coming day, I emptied the coffee dregs into the slop pail, and we went to bed.

Dick had taken the day off for the job interview but set off for work again the next morning in darkness, carrying his lunch in his backpack, as usual.

My day dragged. I baked bread, cast a listless fishing line with no luck, and did some work in my garden. I was bored and depressed with the gloomy fall day and eager to get on with our new life. When I heard the sound of Dick's motor chugging down the lake, I was happy.

I took the lid from the Dutch oven, stirred the chili, and turned to greet Dick as he came through the door, but my greeting died in my throat. Dick had a strange look on his face.

"What's wrong?" I asked, a shiver running down my spine. "What happened?"

"My backpack," he said, sitting down with a thump. "It's gone!"

"What?" I didn't understand.

"A bear stole my backpack," he said, taking off his jacket. "Every morning I hang it from a nail in a tree. Today I was gone for maybe twenty minutes, came back, and it had disappeared. Nothing but a claw mark under the nail."

I set down the Dutch oven lid. "A bear?"

"Believe it." He said, his eyes focusing on the Dutch oven and food. "The pack's gone. I hope the bear liked my peanut butter sandwiches. I'm starving."

He washed his hands in the warm water sitting in its basin on the wood stove. "Craziest thing that's happened so far this year." He shook his head.

I set two bowls of steaming chili on the table, and Dick sat again and lifted a spoonful of chili to his mouth.

"I'm so hungry I could eat the tabletop."

He wolfed down several mouthfuls, then told his story. "Like always, my driver's license and Social Security number were in that pack, not to mention the handgun." He gave a sigh. "That gun was so nice, remember, with the black walnut grips I added to it? Even inlaid them with silver. It was a beauty."

He continued. "Well, I figured my pack should be easy to find. It's got to be near the drilling rig. Right? Fred and I took as much time off from work as we dared to look for it but found nothing. It just disappeared."

"Would it help if I came with you in the morning, and we took a good long look? It's the beginning of your long weekend."

He sighed. "That's not really how I want to spend my day off, and I'm not so sure we'd find anything. A bear can cover a lot of ground in a short time." He sighed again. "But I suppose you're right. We really should give it one more try."

The next morning we arrived at the drilling site, two hundred yards off the Gunflint Trail, before nine. We searched everywhere, moved aside large boughs, ducked under tall spruce trees, shuffled through long grass, and kicked up fallen leaves, making ever-widening circles through the brush. Dick got down on his hands and knees more than once to follow game trails.

We gave Nooky free reign and followed her when she took little forays into the forest, hoping she might have caught the bear's scent. She snuffled and sniffed and had a wonderful time with all sorts of intriguing smells but led us to nothing. The sun rose higher. The air grew hot.

I had stopped to lean against a birch tree, starting to believe this truly was a lost cause, when Dick's voice echoed through the trees. "Come over here!"

I felt a surge of hope. "Find it?" I shouted, stumbling over a dead log,

"Just come!" he yelled. I ran toward the sound of his voice and reached him standing near a mossy hummock a few feet into the underbrush. He pointed down. "You won't believe this!"

I looked and did a double-take. "I *don't* believe it!"

Nestled among the fallen yellow leaves lay a green plastic bag. It was the same one I'd filled with peanut butter sandwiches for Dick's lunch only yesterday. The bag rested in the middle of a large black blob of bear poop. No further detective work required.

"He enjoyed my lunch," Dick grumbled, "but where's my gun and driver's license? And where's my Social Security card? Where's my backpack?"

"He ate them?" I ventured a guess. "Well, not the gun."

We searched for another hour, but as the sun climbed to its zenith and started its descent, we finally decided to call it quits and went home empty handed.

Somewhere in the Superior National Forest a bear was roaming with a driver's license, a Social Security number, and a gun.

47

A Place Near Town

Following the vehicle ahead of me, I turned the Bronco onto a dusty road and continued through the woods up a hill. I was on my way to view a rental house owned by an elderly lady with a heart condition who was now living with family in the Twin Cities. Her niece had agreed to show me the property.

She turned again onto a narrow driveway. I followed and almost hit the brakes as I took in the scene that had opened up ahead of me; the driveway led to an unassuming house, but the view of Lake Superior shimmering in the distance was spectacular.

Although the Maple Hill area was well known to locals, I had no idea it existed. After luxuriating in Tucker Lake's beauty for over a year, I hadn't dared to hope for another lovely spot, especially when renting. But this view was wonderful. I crossed my fingers, hoping the house was decent.

On the lower side of the driveway lay another surprise: a large rectangular garden facing the southern sun, with soil that looked black and loamy. Oh what I could do with a plot like that! Carrots, beans, lettuce. My imagination went wild as I pulled into the parking area in front of the house, at which point my eyes were drawn to another garden on the upper side of the driveway. How lucky could I be?

The niece stepped from her car and saw the direction of my glance. "Potato patch," she said. "Soil up here is wonderful for potatoes, and Auntie got some great harvests."

I was thrilled. I'd worked all summer at my tiny non-productive garden in the woods and here were two ready-made plots! If the house was halfway decent, the gardens would be my reward for this summer's futile efforts.

I followed the woman up an old sidewalk, under a Balm of Gilead tree, and into the house, where the first thing I noticed was a frayed carpet partially covering an uneven floor. Shaking off a stab of disappointment, I looked around, getting a feel for the place, trying to imprint everything so I could report accurately back to Dick: a large living room, a master bedroom, a small guest room, and a good-sized kitchen. Older but useable furniture. Still, it was obvious the house needed upkeep.

So far, my attention had focused on floors and furniture. Now I looked up and suddenly everything changed. Why hadn't I noticed it right away? The view was spectacular. A three-sided panorama of Lake Superior filled the living room windows, and when I opened the door to the master bedroom, the same vista of red maple trees and distant shining blue spread before me. "You can see Isle Royale on a clear day," the niece pointed out.

I squinted. "I can...yes," I muttered, seeing a darker blue patch on the horizon. "Amazing." The lake itself was three miles away.

I tried to focus on my task—finding a decent place to live that didn't cost an arm and a leg—but the stunning view distracted me.

The niece marched into the kitchen. "See how nice and roomy it is." She opened a cupboard. "And lots of storage space."

"And good counter space," I said. "And a view while I'm washing dishes," I added, noting the window over the sink.

"Where does *that* go?" I pointed to a door at the other end of the kitchen.

"To the back entry," she opened it, "and the cellar." She pointed to a stairway leading down.

I stepped into the entryway, noting that the cement blocks forming the walls were crumbly and uneven. (Later this would allow snow to drift in and under the kitchen door. But how was I to know that now?)

Following the niece down the worn cement steps to check out the basement, I stepped onto a dirt floor. That was a disappointment. I looked across the room where several small animal-size holes breeched the foundation's integrity. Not good. Easy access for small wild critters.

Trying to be optimistic, I continued my inspection, stopping when I reached a wall of shelves. They were crammed with jar upon jar of canned green beans and carrots and home-made jams and jellies. I took a closer look. All were labeled at least four years ago. Too old.

This rough basement wasn't a big selling point, and disappointment began to crowd out my earlier excitement. Why did it have to be such a ruin? Trudging up the cellar stairs, I again noticed their dilapidated condition and felt a lump in my throat. Damn. I loved the location and view, but the house's disrepair made this rental a dicey prospect. I should tell the niece the house wasn't right for us and leave. She was a nice lady. I shouldn't waste any more of her time.

With my mind made up, I reentered the kitchen. Because it was open to the living room, the spectacular view of Lake Superior struck me again. Wow. What a sight. Imagine seeing it all day. My doubts and disappointments dimmed, and as I walked across the room, they retreated even more. "You can actually see the lake from back here," I said, my enthusiasm building again as impressions of the dungeonlike basement faded. Who needs a basement, anyway?

I tried to be practical. I really did. For the next half hour, I roamed over the property, looking at a small outside shed, noting the apple tree near the lower garden. I made a mental note of pros and cons, trying to be impartial: the pros were the reasonable rent, the privacy, the wonderful gardens. I could save money by growing tons of produce. And the view.

The cons were obvious: a shabby, older house and a creepy, disintegrating basement. But, I reasoned with myself, the living spaces weren't *that* bad.

Finally, I made the decision. "I'll take it. But we can't move in for a few weeks. Well, we're not sure when but sometime in October." Hauling out my fringed macramé purse, I took out my checkbook and wrote a check for the down payment on the rental.

She thanked me, handed me a set of keys, got in her car, and drove off. I took another moment to look around, hoping I'd made the right decision. Yet I'd known from the minute I glimpsed that panoramic view, I'd take the place. Pleased with myself, I hopped into the car and headed back down the driveway, oblivious to the northwest breeze that was even now wafting in the front window, a breeze that, in winter, would escalate into gale-force gusts that would shake the very foundations of the house. Nor had it occurred to me that the *very* long driveway would be packed with drifts of wind-driven snow all winter. All I saw was the spectacular view. I couldn't wait to tell Dick about the great place with the wonderful vista that would be our new home.

48

EVERYTHING MOVED TOO FAST

Suddenly life started to move with lightning speed. I felt like a leaf carried down the spring crest of the Tucker River.

Dick's drilling job ended without fanfare. He and Fred took down the rig, shook a friendly good-bye, and Fred went back to his home on the Iron Range.

Dick and I spent the next day working around the cabin, snugging up the place in preparation for our departure. We planned to move to Maple Hill the following week, and Dick had been told his new job would began the week after that.

The second morning after the drilling job ended, Dick announced he needed lumber to shim up the floor and had to make a trip to Grand Marais.

"Hey, I'll go along and show you the house on Maple Hill," I said.

Several hours later we pulled into the rental house driveway, and a pall of disappointment fell over me. The old house looked more dilapidated than I remembered. It didn't help that a hazy fog obliterated the fantastic view of Lake Superior. Still, I tried to be optimistic. "The other day I could actually see Isle Royale in the distance. It was quite a view," I said.

Dick had other things on his mind. "Is there a well some-where?"

I pointed to a weed-filled patch as we got out of the car. "Yeah. It's in there. Let's go inside." If only the fog would lift, he'd be blown over by the panoramic view from the living room windows.

I inserted the key, but the door wouldn't budge. I tried again. No luck. Frustrated, I tried again, but something was sticking. Dick's introduction to this place was not going well. I took a deep breath, gave a hefty push, and as the door swung open I halfway fell into the living room.

Dick inspected the door lock. "This needs a little work."

"Look!" I pointed at the spectacular living room view now obliterated by fog. "It's really something. You'll see," I promised.

"I believe you," he said after a brief look. "How's the place heated?"

"Fuel oil. Radiators with water."

"Hmmm," he said.

I pointed out the bedrooms and kitchen, and when he asked about the basement I glossed over it. "Kind of a cellar," I said.

"Show me." Rats. He wanted to see. As I led him down the steps, I murmured, "It's a bit rough down here."

At the bottom he viewed the useless canned goods and open spaces in the foundation. "I'll say," was his only comment.

"We won't live here forever," I pointed out. "And the gar-dens will be great." We traipsed back upstairs, where he again viewed the bedrooms and the kitchen. "It's okay," he said. "Any-way, you've paid the rent and we're committed, so this'll be our new home for a while."

Disappointed that the view I loved had been obliterated by fog, I followed Dick to our vehicle and we headed for town. Speeding down the Gunflint hill to Grand Marais, we discussed what furniture we needed, possible kitchen utensils, and the fact I'd have to continue using the laundromat in town.

We lunched at the El Ray café, located downtown across the street from Joynes. As we paid our bill, we bumped into the manager of Arrowhead Electric. Following a flurry of greetings, Dick asked when he should report for work.

"Glad I ran into you," said the manager. "Plans have changed, and I need you tomorrow. Can you do it?" My heart sank. What was this? We'd been told we had another two weeks.

I was upset, and I left the two men as they discussed details to wait in the car. An uprooted sensation filled me. All our plans had to be changed. We'd hoped to move to Maple Hill before Dick started his new job. Now, he'd have to commute from Tucker again. Only this time, he have to canoe over two lakes and a portage, then drive an additional fifty-seven miles to the work site.

"What's the deal?" I asked a few minutes later when Dick got in the car. "I thought we had more time."

"He saw me before he had a chance to leave a message at Loon Lake. Apparently I'm working for a subcontractor clearing a new line east of Grand Marais, and everything is set to start, so I need to be there."

I wasn't happy, but we needed this job.

"That means a hundred miles round-trip every day, not to mention traveling over the lakes," I said.

"More than that," Dick corrected me. "It's fifty-seven miles one way. But it's only four days. Then I get a week off so we can move."

We stopped at Hedstrom's and bought the lumber Dick needed, then headed home. A ton of chores awaited us as the future began closing in. Packing to move, securing our little log dock, and snugging up the cabin were foremost on our to-do list. I wasn't morose, but I didn't feel like cheerleading either.

When we arrived at the cabin, a flutter of gray feathers told me the gray jays were waiting in the bushes. My heart always warmed at the sight of them, and to cheer myself up I ran inside and retrieved a few chunks of bread from a sourdough loaf.

Bonnie sat on a moose maple branch and, as always, waited for me to toss her the treats. She swooped down to grab a few pieces and disappeared into the woods. Clyde sat in a hazel bush thicket. I held my hand palm-up, offering bread, and waited for him to land and take the food as he always did. Usually he kept coming back as long as I fed him.

Not today. Clyde clung to his low-hanging branch. Normally he chirped out soft "chunk-chunks," but today he was silent.

"Dick," I caught his attention as he carried the life jackets into the cabin. "What's with Clyde? He's acting strange."

Dick halted and took a long look. "He doesn't look good."

He didn't. Usually perky, Clyde now seemed bedraggled. His wings looked unkempt, and his chest feathers were ruffled instead of smooth. Normally, his lively eyes followed our every move as we fed him. Today they were dull.

But the most alarming thing was that he wasn't flying to my hand to eat. That was very unusual. "Throw the bread on the ground," Dick suggested.

I tossed several hunks in front of me, and Clyde dropped awkwardly to the ground, took the bread, and flew off into the woods.

"That was weird," I said, as we turned to go inside.

Everything was changing too fast.

49

An Even Longer Commute

Four thirty the next morning came much too soon. In the cold autumn dark, I sent Dick off to his new job. He carried a huge lunch: thick peanut butter sandwiches on homemade bread, half a dozen chocolate chip cookies, and a thermos of steaming hot coffee. He'd need all the energy he could muster for the long day ahead.

As I watched, he stepped into the canoe, started the motor, and disappeared into the black morning, the four-horsepower motor putt-putting down the lake. Sighing, I picked up the broom for a daily sweeping of the floor. We might be moving soon, but that was no reason to be a slob.

As I swept up tufts of dog hair, leaves, and bits of kindling, I thought about my garden. Although a failure by most standards, I'd poured my heart and soul into it, working the soil, adding every smidge of organic matter I could find, and carefully tending it. With a jolt, I realized that leaving my garden was going to be the hardest part of moving from Tucker Lake.

How could I abandon it? I sat at the kitchen table, looked

out over the lake and the autumn yellow trees, and thought about my garden.

I'll work in it today, I resolved, and give it a final going over. The thought made me feel better immediately. I'd spread the coffee grounds and eggshells from the compost container, then work the soil one last time. It wasn't as if we were leaving forever. Next spring I'd plant carrots and potatoes and tend it on weekends. I simply couldn't abandon it in the forest without a future. I had to believe I'd come back.

Later in the morning, after finishing chores, I picked up the hoe and walked to my tiny plot. Nooky followed. She sat and watched for a while, then disappeared behind the biffy, snuffling and sniffing.

I threw the organic material onto the soil and worked it in. It didn't take long, but during my brief flurry of garden activity my sadness disappeared. Finally, nothing remained to do; I took the hoe in hand and started walking back to the cabin.

Suddenly a loud growl sounded from somewhere behind the biffy. I stopped. It was Nooky's moose growl. Turning towards the noise, I quickened my pace and ran towards the outhouse. Not another moose!

Reaching the outhouse, I scanned the area. Nothing. Yet Nooky's barks grew louder and more enraged. This wasn't good. I gripped the hoe and wished I had the shotgun.

Another sound from farther away caught my attention—a clanging, clunking noise. I was trying to figure it out when suddenly Nooky burst over the hill. Barking at the top of her lungs, she stopped and turned to growl in the direction from which she'd just come.

Perplexed, I peered into the woods. The strange clanking noise continued. What was it? Something metallic? For the life of me, I couldn't figure it out.

"C'mon, Nooky," I called. She'd stopped some twenty feet from me but paid no attention to my call, didn't even look my way.

"Come!" I yelled, but she kept barking at something just beyond the tree line. I retreated to the back of the cabin, where I could quickly jump on the deck to safety. Nooky didn't follow, but instead ran forward towards the clanking noise.

Just then an enormous bull moose crested the hill, his tremendous rack clanging and crashing against trees, pushing aside saplings. My mouth dropped. It looked impossible for the animal to navigate the thick woods with so large a rack, but he was doing just fine.

Nooky's barking frenzy hit a new high. I thought back to early summer when she'd relentlessly badgered the mother moose, forcing her to take refuge in the lake along with her tiny calf. But this was no cow moose. This was a huge bull, and it was rutting season, which makes these guys testy. Nooky had more than met her match.

To my dismay, the huge brown hulk of a moose shifted his course slightly and started moving in the direction of the cabin. "No, no, no, no," I whispered. This was not good. He couldn't come this way. No.

Was he just blundering about, or was he intent on shutting up my yappy dog? I panicked. Moose have notoriously bad eyesight. Maybe he didn't see the cabin. What would happen if he clunked into it?

I wished Nooky would stop her incessant barking. What should I do? This one-ton creature was veering directly towards my home, and my dog stood in the way. Time to take charge. I'm the human. I'm supposed to be a member of an intelligent species. Right?

The only thing I could think of was to make noise. A few days ago my yells had chased a lady moose from my garden. But why, my panicked brain asked, were so many moose traipsing across my territory?

No sense wasting time wondering. Action was needed. I took a breath and, once again, put my deep, loud voice to good use. "GO! GET!" I yelled at the top of my lungs, trying to sound fierce. I continued repeating myself, booming out in the deepest bass I could muster. "Get out of here! Stop all this nonsense!"

The moose and Nooky ignored me.

Taking a deeper breath, I yelled at the moose, "GET OUT OF HERE." Once more, this time at the dog. "NOOKY! COME! COME!" I yelled at the sky. I shouted at the lake. I made as much noise as humanly possible.

My yelling tactic didn't seem to be working. I was about to despair. And then, suddenly, without preamble, the enormous bull gave its huge head and rack a final gigantic shake and veered off towards the north. Feeling a huge sense of relief, I listened as his clanging rack reverberated through the forest as he slowly—too slowly—disappeared.

Nooky stood near the biffy in guard-dog mode until the moose noise was a distant rattle and snap of underbrush. Then she ran over to me, tail wagging, proud of her performance.

"You did okay, Nooks, but you've got to stop challenging moose. They're too big for you." Relieved that the huge creature had gone, I sat down on the deck, suddenly exhausted. Nooky lay beside me, and I scratched under her collar and around her ears while we listened to the silence.

The only sound was the distant "wank" of nuthatches. The peace and quiet felt good. My tension ebbed away, and Nooky fell asleep. I hoped the rest of the day would be uneventful, even boring, and started thinking about my next chore. I lifted my face to drink in the sun rays, and a soft "chunk-chunk" caught my attention.

Opening my eyes, I recognized the familiar blur of gray wings in the underbrush. My birds! I ran inside and grabbed bacon bits I'd saved for the gray jays.

I threw tidbits to Bonnie, easily recognizable by her smaller size and shy demeanor, but Clyde was nowhere to be seen.

A whirr of wings flapped near my head. "Clyde!" I cried

and turned to offer him a bacon bit. But it wasn't Clyde. It was the young bird that Bonnie and Clyde sometimes brought with them—the bird we'd dubbed C.W. He had never before come to me for food, but always waited in the underbrush for his parents to feed him.

Would he let me feed him today? I held out my hand.

Sure enough, he landed, took the treat, and flew away much as his father had done.

This was something new. I couldn't wait to tell Dick, but as I threw more scraps for Bonnie and offered several more tidbits to C.W., I continued to wonder what happened to Clyde. Was he dead?

50

GOOD-BYE TUCKER LAKE

The day we ended our year in the woods was drizzly. Raindrops slid down the window panes. We could almost feel the leaden sky, a heavy gray pushing down on us.

I welcomed the gloom. Yesterday had been golden, with birch and poplar shining yellow on the hill across the lake, the sky a burnished blue. Today's dreariness made it easier to leave, and that surprised me. I thought I was happy to be leaving.

Dick had finished the four long days of working for Arrowhead Electric and now had a week off. During this time we planned to bring our meager belongings to the rental house and visit our families in the Twin Cities, collect lamps, rugs, and kitchen utensils that we'd stored with our parents, and complete our move into our place on Maple Hill.

The move would mean that we'd have to deal with the details of modern existence again that we'd left behind when we moved to Tucker Lake: install a phone and get a number, make sure the power was hooked up, get a new mailing address. Dick would start his job the following Monday, and we'd begin a new life. Exactly how things would turn out was still an open question, but I was okay with that.

At least I thought I was. The last two weeks on Tucker had found me restless and antsy to move on. I was ready. However, today as I packed and lugged everything to the canoe, each item seemed to hold a memory; the wool long underwear I'd been forced to buy at Joynes when the fall weather got colder and my fashionable city jeans weren't warm enough; the candy thermometer we'd used on so many frigid, fudge-making evenings; even the durable spatula I'd used every morning when frying eggs. I couldn't leave any of these items behind.

As the packing chores dwindled I was surprised by an overwhelming wave of sadness. How would we earn a living? Would we make new friends? Would a couple of city kids like us enjoy life in rural northern Minnesota? I hoped the beauty and power of Lake Superior and the wildness of the Superior National Forest would fill me with the same inner peace and well-being I'd found at Tucker Lake.

We finished our tasks, Dick working with chainsaw and tools, I with household items. And suddenly, it was time to go. Except—"I need to sweep the floor," I told Dick. He nodded with a quizzical look, which I ignored. I ran back to the cabin. I couldn't leave until I said good-bye to it, and I had to be alone for that.

Grabbing the broom, I pushed it across the floor, giving my little cabin one more sweep, and thought of how I'd changed in the past year. From a city woman who'd taken pride in her spotlessly clean apartment to someone who loved this small cabin with its plywood floor.

I wiped the dusty ashes from the fireplace top, remembering how we struggled when installing it, placing cobblestones in the rapidly drying cement. It had been one of many feats that made me physically stronger—a side benefit of wilderness life.

I straightened the kerosene lamp resting on the kitchen cabinet, recalling the excitement of our first morning coffee in the new kitchen. So many precious memories filled the air in this tiny building. But it was time to go. The fire was out, the cabin chilly.

This place, so full of life, was about to become a barren lake cabin again, a place to be visited on weekends and vacations. We were leaving it cold and empty. I set the broom in its place in the corner and went out the door with a tight throat.

Moving down the steps at a snail's pace, I tossed a few tidbits on the ground for the birds. C.W. and Bonnie would find my farewell breakfast. They'd been returning regularly, but Clyde hadn't been back since the day we first noticed his disheveled appearance. My gut told me his time had come.

I squared my shoulders, took a deep breath, and turned toward the canoe, where Dick stood waiting.

Arranging myself in the canoe's prow with Nooky at my feet, surrounded by plastic garbage cans filled with books, kitchen utensils, and spices, I looked up at the bleak sky. Dick had just started pulling the motor cord when I yelled. " Stop! I forgot Nooky's ladybug! We can't leave that."

Dick stilled the starter cord, and I jumped from the canoe. Racing to the deck, I stooped down and grabbed the pink ladybug from Nooky's dusty lair.

"We can't start a new life without this," I said as I tucked it into a duffel bag.

Finally, our jam-packed canoe moved away from the dock, and we slowly putted out onto the lake. Through a veil of drizzle, I watched our cabin grow smaller in the distance. Just before it disappeared around the bend, flashes of gray caught my eye.

The gray jays were coming for their hand-outs, but we wouldn't be there to enjoy them.

Epilogue

We have spent the last fifty years on the North Shore of Lake Superior, in close proximity to Minnesota's border country wilderness. We built several businesses during that time and worked hard, but we have never regretted moving here. We raised two children, Betsy and Tom, and became part of the community.

We built a cabin and then a house on an inland lake near Grand Marais.

We still own and visit our parcel of land on Tucker Lake, although our beloved little cabin had to be razed due to survey issues with the federal government. My wish is that our descendants will love this patch of wilderness as much as we do.

Joan Crosby lives near Grand Marais, Minnesota, with her husband, Dick, and her beloved pug, Mr. Magoo. She has been a columnist for the *Cook County News Herald* for the past two decades. A graduate of the University of Minnesota, Joan has also sold real estate and taught high school English and adult education. She loves the outdoors, street rods, gardening, visiting the Ozarks in the springtime, and, of course, writing.

Fifty years ago, she and her husband, Dick, moved from Minneapolis to spend a winter on the outskirts of the BWCA in a primitive cabin without road access or modern conveniences. That experience is the subject of this book.